I0829933

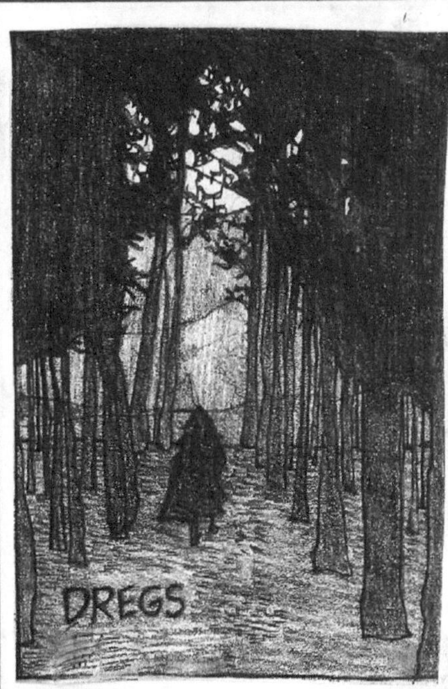
DREGS

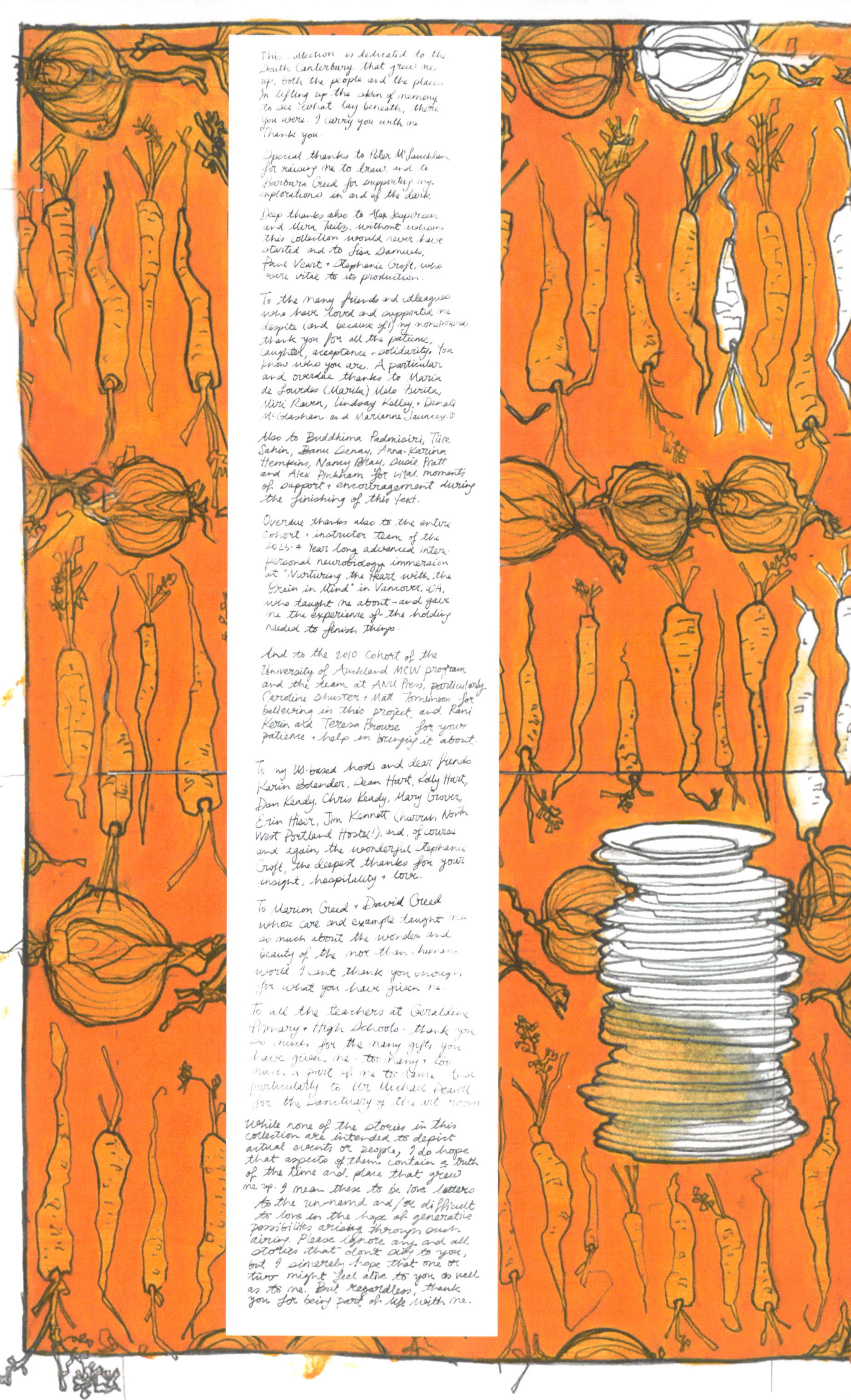

This collection is dedicated to the South Canterbury that grew me up, both the people and the places. In lifting up the skin of memory to see what lay beneath, there you were. I carry you with me. Thank you.

Special thanks to Peter McLauchlan, for raising me to draw, and to Barbara Creed for supporting my explorations in and of the dark.

Deep thanks also to Alex Jasprizza and Mira Taitz, without whom this collection would never have started, and to Lisa Samuels, Paul Veart + Stephanie Croft, who were vital to its production.

To the many friends and colleagues who have loved and supported me despite (and because of!) my nonsense, thank you for all the patience, laughter, acceptance + solidarity. You know who you are. A particular and overdue thanks to Maria de Lourdes (Marilu) Melo Zurita, Miri Raven, Lindsay Kelley, + Denali McGlashan and Marianne Jauncey.

Also to Buddhima Padmasiri, Türe Sahin, Banu Senay, Anna-Katrina Hempkins, Nancy Blay, Susie Pratt and Alex Pinkham for vital moments of support + encouragement during the finishing of this text.

Overdue thanks also to the entire cohort + instructor team of the 2023-4 year long advanced interpersonal neurobiology immersion at "Nurturing the Heart with the Brain in Mind" in Vancouver, WA, who taught me about - and gave me the experience of - the holding needed to finish things.

And to the 2010 cohort of the University of Auckland MCW program and the team at ANU Press, particularly Caroline Shuster + Matt Tomlinson for believing in this project, and Rani Kerin and Teresa Prowse for your patience + help in bringing it about.

To my US-based hosts and dear friends Karin Bolender, Dean Hart, Kelly Hart, Dan Keady, Chris Keady, Mary Grover, Erin Hiser, Jim Kennett Churrah North West Portland Hostel(!), and, of course and again the wonderful Stephanie Croft, who deepest thanks for your insight, hospitality + love.

To Marion Creed + David Creed whose care and example taught me so much about the wonder and beauty of the more-than-human world. I can't thank you enough for what you have given me.

To all the teachers at Geraldine Primary + High Schools - thank you so much for the many gifts you have given me - too many + too much a part of me to name. But particularly to Mr Michael Pearce for the sanctuary of the art room.

While none of the stories in this collection are intended to depict actual events or people, I do hope that aspects of them contain a truth of the time and place that grew me up. I mean these to be love letters to the un-named and/or difficult to love in the hope of generative possibilities arising through such airing. Please ignore any and all stories that don't add up to you, but I sincerely hope that one or two might feel alive to you as well as to me. But regardless, thank you for being part of life with me.

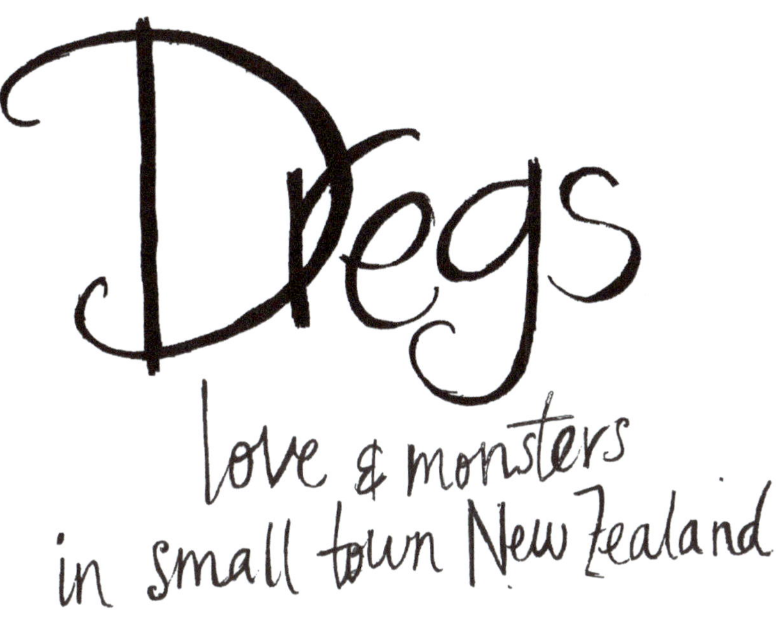

Dregs

Love & monsters in small town New Zealand

Laura McLauchlan

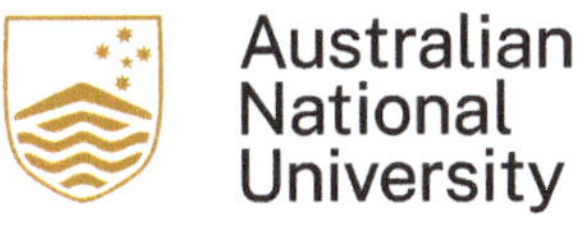

Australian
National
University

ANU PRESS

MONOGRAPHS IN
ANTHROPOLOGY SERIES

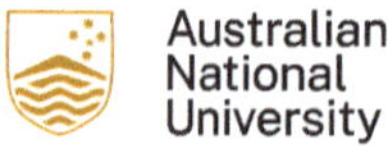

ANU PRESS

Published by ANU Press
The Australian National University
Canberra ACT 2600, Australia
Email: anupress@anu.edu.au

Available to download for free at press.anu.edu.au

ISBN (print): 9781760466657
ISBN (online): 9781760466664

WorldCat (print): 1457056280
WorldCat (online): 1457056455

DOI: 10.22459/D.2024

Cover and all illustrations by Laura McLauchlan
Design and layout by ANU Press and Laura McLauchlan

This book is published under the aegis of the Anthropology in Pacific and Asian Studies editorial board of ANU Press.

Publication of this book has been supported by the ANU vice-chancellor's strategic funds for flagship titles at ANU Press.

CONTENTS

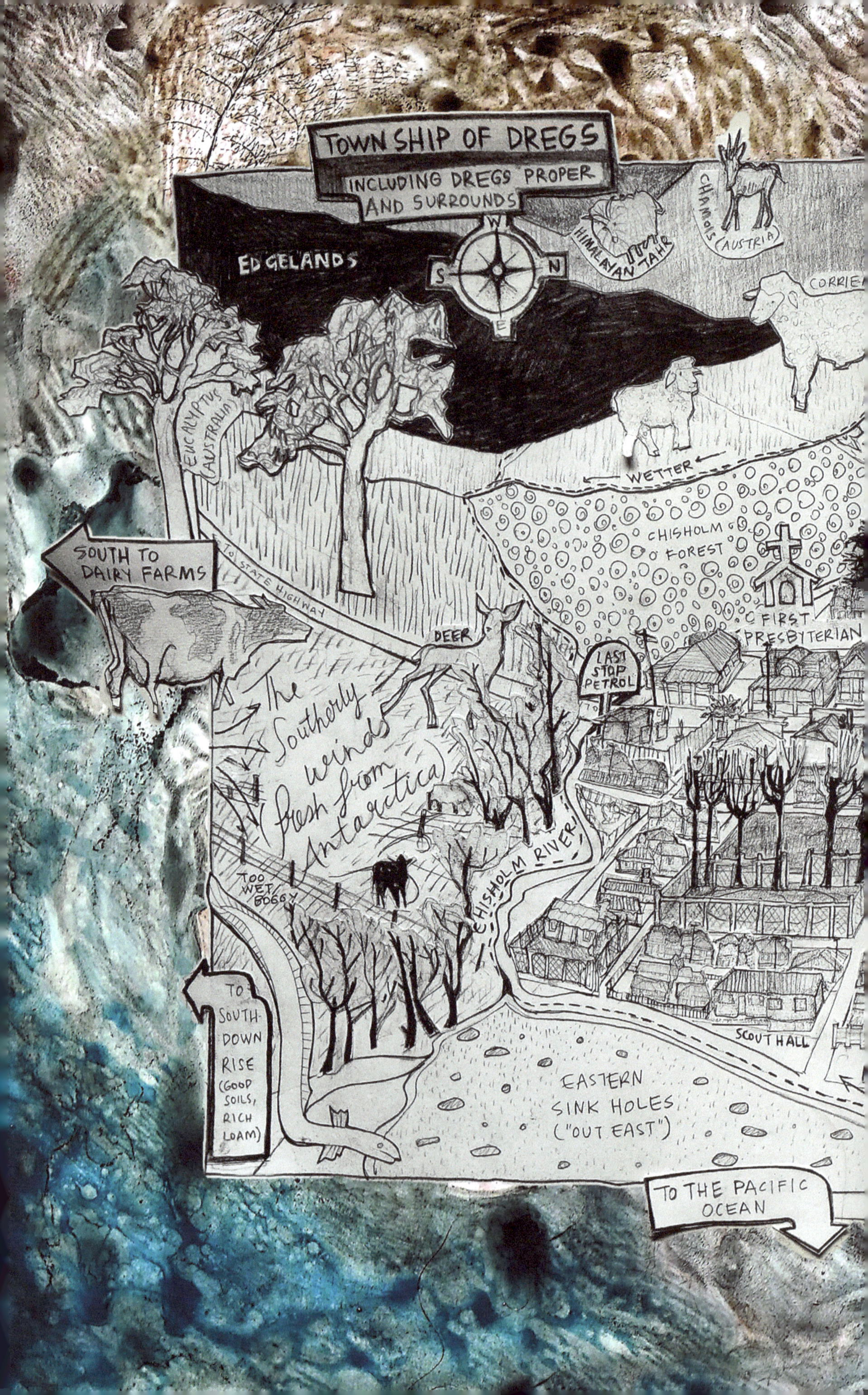

TOWNSHIP OF DREGS
INCLUDING DREGS PROPER AND SURROUNDS
EDGELANDS
HIMALAYAN TAHR
CHAMOIS (AUSTRIA)
CORRIE
EUCALYPTUS (AUSTRALIA)
WETTER
CHISHOLM FOREST
SOUTH TO DAIRY FARMS
TO STATE HIGHWAY
FIRST PRESBYTERIAN
DEER
LAST STOP PETROL
The Southerly winds from Antarctica
CHISHOLM RIVER
TOO WET BOGGY
SCOUT HALL
TO SOUTH DOWN RISE (GOOD SOILS, RICH LOAM)
EASTERN SINK HOLES ("OUT EAST")
TO THE PACIFIC OCEAN

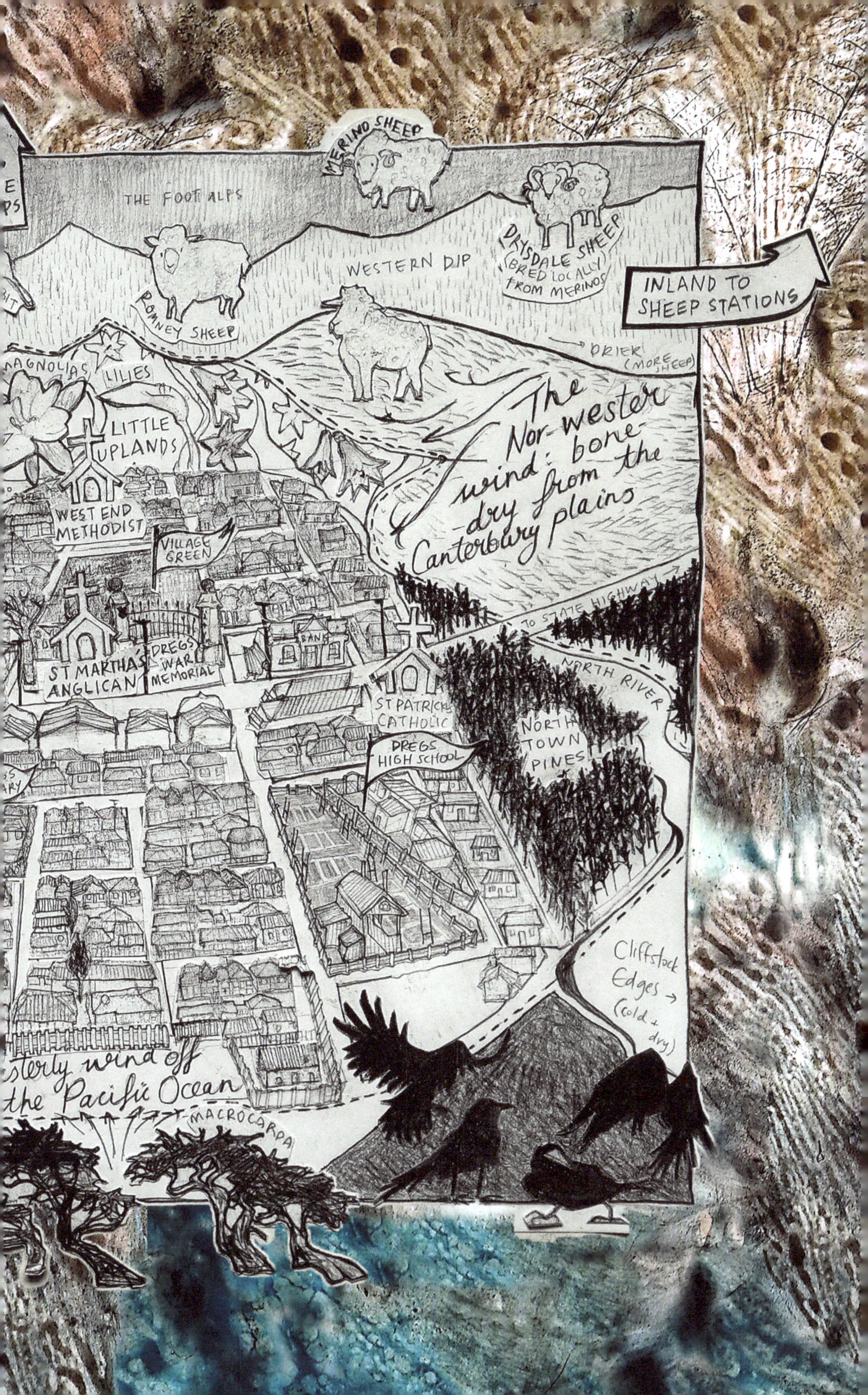

MERINO SHEEP
THE FOOT ALPS
WESTERN DIP
DRYSDALE SHEEP (BRED LOCALLY FROM MERINOS)
INLAND TO SHEEP STATIONS
ROMNEY SHEEP
DRIER (MORE SHEEP)
MAGNOLIAS
LILIES
LITTLE UPLANDS
WEST END METHODIST
VILLAGE GREEN
The Nor-wester wind: bone-dry from the Canterbury plains
TO STATE HIGHWAY 7
NORTH RIVER
ST MARTHAS ANGLICAN
DREGS WAR MEMORIAL
BANK
ST PATRICKS CATHOLIC
DREGS HIGH SCHOOL
NORTH TOWN PINES
Cliffstock Edges (cold + dry)
...sterly wind off the Pacific Ocean
MACROCARPA

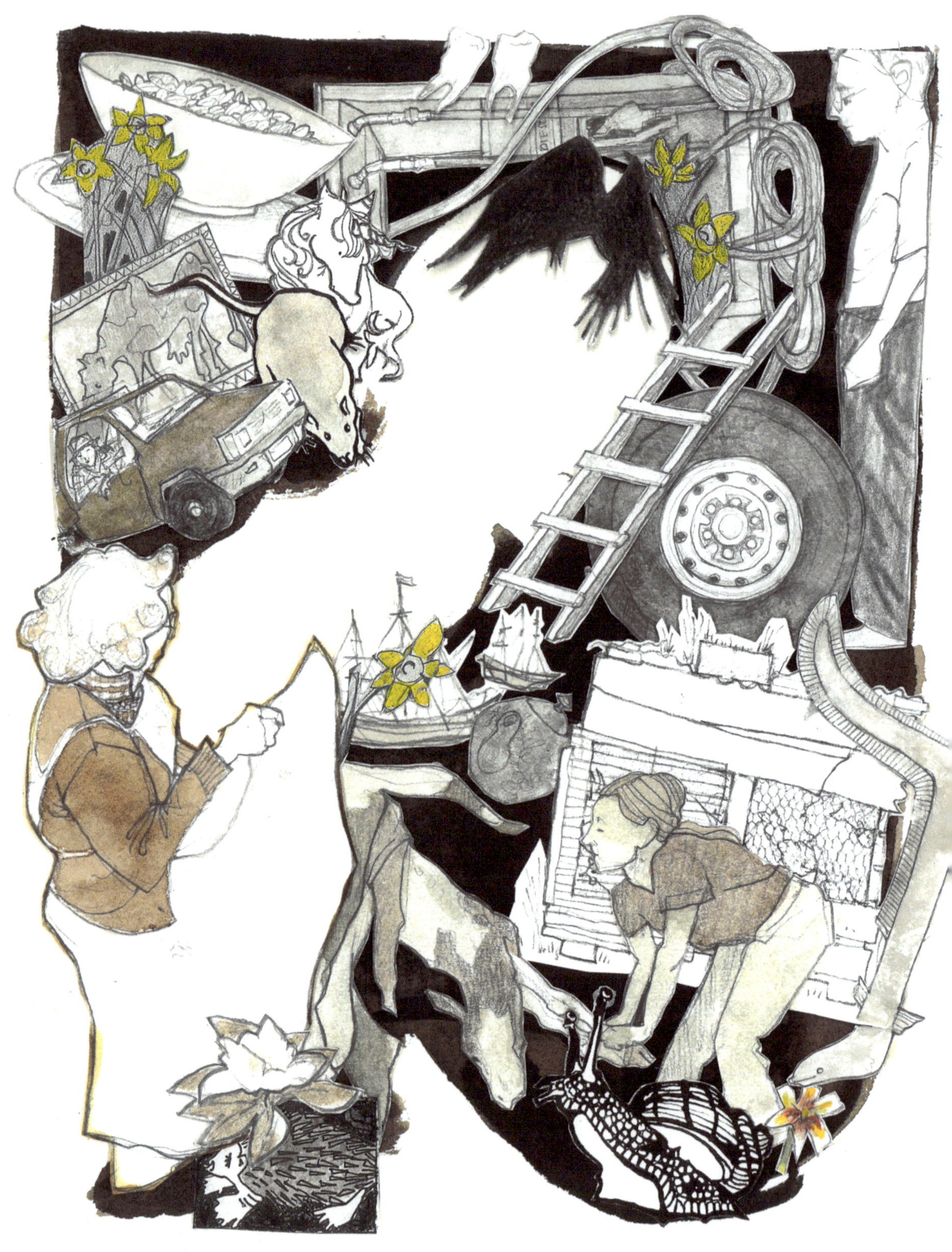

Introduction

> To worry or to smile, such is the choice when we are assailed by
> the strange; our decision depends on how familiar we are with our
> own ghosts.
>
> (Kristeva 1991, 191)

This collection started 13 years ago, driven by my fascination with the
monstrous feminine. I hadn't initially meant for these stories to also be
an exploration of rural New Zealand life. In writing what I knew of the
feminine monstrous, however, the entities that I dredged up came coupled
with the landscapes and social worlds of the places that grew me up.
And so the collection became about the monsters of a specific place and
time—a largely farming area on the eastern side of Te Waipounamu, the
South Island of Aotearoa/New Zealand in the 1990s.

The genuine charm—and even quaintness—of the towns of this bucolic
region that colonial settlers called 'South Canterbury' might make
them seem unlikely places to find the monstrous. Many of the towns
in the region, including my own hometown, Geraldine, are famously
pretty, characterised by diverse farmlands, often lush rivers, green
foothills, charming parks and architecture, and a backdrop of rugged
mountainscapes. However, as anthropologist of monsters Yasmine
Musharbash notes, monsters are entities with 'a defiant relationship to
order', emerging from the crossing of boundaries and defying cultural
categories and taboos (Musharbash 2023, 1). The social rules—both spoken
and not—that supported the pretty landscapes and pleasant lifeways of
these places thus provide fertile ground for the monstrous.

Dregs—the town in which this collection of stories is set—is not a
pseudonym for any particular South Canterbury town. Instead, I imagine
Dregs as a shadow twin of a conglomerate of towns in the region. Here,
following my own felt sense of various lines of taboo, Dregs is home to
beings who live on the edges of a host of cultural boundaries—sexual,
gendered, racialised, classed, religious and even species boundaries.
These tales—and their monsters—are particular and limited, reflecting the
lifeways of a largely pākehā (non-Māori of European ancestry) populated
small town in the 1990s, as told and drawn by a pākehā, queer and able-
bodied woman of Protestant descent. These lands were, and remain, the
takiwā, or territory, of Kāi Tahu, the principle iwi (tribe) of Te Waipounamu.
In acknowledging the situatedness of my knowledge (Haraway 1988), it
becomes clear that, while I hope for these fictional stories to reflect *a* truth
of the time and place that grew me up, such stories can only tell one very

particular view of life and monsters in such places. In order to more fully story the lands and times within which these tales and sketches are set, other stories from other tellers are needed and may need different fora in order to speak and be heard with power (Smith et al. 2002, 171). I hope that, in sharing the disconnections and limits of the colonial worlds that are part of me, that this collection will help demonstrate the necessity for shifts of power and voice.

While these stories and sketches belong to a very specific place and time, I hope that these gestures towards the tender monstrous might offer a moment of curiosity about the monsters of the reader's own hometown or city, wherever that might be, and perhaps even a consideration of how one might better live alongside such radical others. And for those who, like me, were grown up by those lands and waters demarcated by the Rangitata River in the north and the Waitaki River to the south, with the Pacific Ocean and Southern Alps forming its eastern and western edges—or perhaps even similar places in other parts of Aotearoa/New Zealand—I am curious to know if you recognise the boundary-transgressing beings who move through these stories and, if you know of others, I would love to hear their stories.

The stories

The stories and sketches that form this collection come from methods of writing and drawing from embodied imagination to explore aspects of life that may not be fully conscious. The collection takes much from Gloria Anzaldúa's celebration of the ways in which bodily knowing arises in response to both external, 'real', events as well as those from the imagination (Anzaldúa 1999, 59–60). While I've spent much of my career as an anthropologist attempting to parse out reality from imagination, this collection celebrates the entanglements of knowing. Through this task of body writing and remembering, smell—a sense undervalued and, at times, itself rendered monstrous in Western imaginaries (Synnott 1991; Giblett 2008)—became a core element of many of the stories. Touch, texture, wetness and dryness also became fixations. Wetness, in particular, seemed to suggest both the aliveness and fertility that emerged in proximity to the monstrous, yet something that could also threaten engulfment. Thus, dryness at times carries a sense of deadness in the stories, while at others something more like relief. The interplay of wet and dry, however, is more felt than theoretically coherent, and I will leave its navigation to the reader. While emerging from a felt sense of lively monstrousness, these fictional stories are also ethnographic in their desire to be 'accountable to the world outside the text' (Narayan 1999, 141)[1]—that is, they intend to reflect not only my inner world (as if any inner world was ever disconnected from the outer), but also to actively trace the economics, gender politics and norms of sexuality, and of animal and human relations among which such monsters emerge and make sense.

All land mammals—human and more-than-human—in Aotearoa/New Zealand have ancestors from elsewhere, with bats being the country's only endemic mammals. Introduced beings do at times cause disastrous trouble in these lands, and I have explored my own stubborn attachment to several such species elsewhere in my academic work (McLauchlan 2024). While not disputing the ecological harms many of us introduced beings cause, *Dregs* as a collection is partly animated by my persistent wondering about which species are recognised as harmful and which are not, as well as what that means for who is considered to belong. Many plants and animals recognised as being harmful to valued ecosystems and farmland were and are referred to as 'introduced', despite their ancestors having arrived more than a century ago to these islands. While the belonging of such beings is questioned, the settler colonial imaginaries I grew up in offered a welcome and a sense of belonging to other species, including ourselves as settler colonial-descended people, and those deemed useful to us, such as sheep, dogs and (not without controversy) cows, regardless of our ecosystemic impact. *Dregs* tells the stories of many beings whose harms tend to be more widely recognised (and their belonging more disputed), including rabbits and eucalypts, but also chamois (from Austria) and Himalayan thar—two introduced species valued locally for hunting as well as being recognised as being damaging to ecosystems. As Park et al. (2002) have argued, such introduced species may even take on an element of the monstrous, with pine trees in Northland being framed by some as 'vampiric'. Possums, pines, magpies, crows and other beings recognised as problematic—and thus also as 'introduced'—move through the stories, sometimes visually, rather than in text.

This collection of stories is also animated by an identifiably 'not from here' being, namely Yukka, the subject of the first story in the collection and who, for me, somehow cracked open the space the other stories required. Like other beings in these stories, Yukka is not unchanged by her journey from elsewhere, and nor is she harmless. I first came to know Yukka through a retelling of her tale in 'The Son of the Ogress' in Barbara Hayes's

---

1   In adopting a fictional approach to an ethnographic goal, these stories gratefully inherit from a number of anthropological works. There has been widespread recognition of ethnographies as texts that actively utilise style and authorial voice in order to achieve their effects since the *Writing Culture* debates of the 1980s (Marcus and Cushman 1982; Clifford and Marcus 1986; Clifford 1983). As Nancy Schmidt notes, anthropologists have been writing novels, short stories, plays and poetry for well over a century—even if they received relatively little scholarly attention at the time of their writing (Schmidt 1984). In the post *Writing Culture* years, the advantages of fiction as an ethnographic form have been explored in greater depth, including the potential for fictional forms to support the exploration of relationships between subjectivities and environments (Laterza 2007; Lyons 2003), as well as for holding contradiction and ambiguity (Sarukkai 1997).

Folk Tales and Fables of the World (1987), illustrated by Robert Ingpen. Hayes identifies the story as being of 'old Indian' origin. As a young reader, I had been captivated by the story of this tragic horse-headed ogre woman, her attempt to catch a brahman husband and, perhaps particularly, her heartbroken desire to give the gift of her powers to her half-human son. Rather than Yukka being her given name, the figure actually *is* a (female) yakkha or yakkhinī (Pāli, corresponding to the Sanskrit यक्षिणी yakṣiṇī/ yakshini), a category of beings who are variously described as female demons, vampires or ogres, but also as nature deities and beings of the forests and wilds. She has no given name in the story in which I first met her, being referred to instead as 'the yakka' (which I would later come to realise was a non-standard spelling of the male yakkha). However, longing for something to call her by, I found myself using a misremembered version of yakka, Yukka, as if it was her first name. Almost 20 years later, I was delighted to meet an earlier version of her story in Theravadan Buddhist studies, where she is part of the Jataka tales of the former lives of the Buddha. In this telling, her reincarnation as a horse-headed female yakkha is a punishment for lying about having committed sins against her husband-king, Brahmadatta, king of Benares; her son, who accepts the gifts of his mother, is one of the former incarnations of the Buddha (Francis 1897). Although in both tellings it is the son, not the mother, who is the focus of the tales, I've always found myself deeply—if uncomfortably— sympathetic to her plight, carrying a sense of this yakkha as a force to live with. Despite being so drawn, I had tried for a time not to include Yukka in these stories, concerned with the issue of appropriating of a tale from another people. Although that issue remains unresolved (and I remain answerable to it), I have not been able to imagine this collection without her, the other stories are somehow unable to make sense to me without Yukka's presence. That she should also seem to demand to be first among the stories is perhaps unsurprising, considering, as one reviewer kindly noted, that yakkhini are often guardians.

The sense of disturbing aliveness that Yukka had for me—a realness that goes beyond the literary—is the tuning fork that guided the process of feeling out other monstrous forces that my body knew but which I had no names for. While Yukka introduces the qualities of the actively threatening and devouring woman most strongly, in giving space for the emergence of other entities that my body recognised as having a Yukka-level of aliveness, those who emerged were often beings who rejected a host of socially sanctioned and, particularly, gendered behaviours. While I was not surprised that many of the male monsters that emerged had a sweetness that I recognised as culturally taboo for its 'feminine' quality, I was somewhat (and perhaps naïvely) surprised at the abundance of monstrous women who emerged; I had imagined that growing up in 'feminist' New Zealand would mean that my body would deem fewer behaviours as monstrously out of the bounds for women. Aspects of female strength and leadership are, in theory, celebrated in Aotearoa/New Zealand, with the country having had three female leaders and being the first nation in the world to achieve universal suffrage. Locally, too, there was room for women's leadership and skill: committees of older women in many ways seemed to run the towns of South Canterbury, providing both the volunteer labour and also, often, the vision behind local festivals and cultural events; neighbouring Otago had had the first women's secondary school in the Southern Hemisphere; and Aotearoa/New Zealand's first woman doctor had come from South Canterbury's own Waimate. Yet womanhood in Aotearoa/New Zealand is often marked by tight balancing acts—with permission granted to be strong and practical but with accompanying unspoken requirements to not be too dominant, or too frightening, or too sexual (just sexual enough, and in socially acceptable ways). The presence of monstrousness emerging from the crossing of such gendered norms, even in just a generative pinch, is in all of the stories.

Despite Aotearoa/New Zealand's own self-image as a nation characterised by freedom and progressive ideals, some scholars have argued that behind this 'brighter Britain' or 'God's own country', was a nation with a 'deeply repressed personality' in which 'the forces of social isolation were many and powerful' (Fairburn 2013, 11).[2] Taboos around sexual and sensual expression animate many aspects of the monstrous in this collection. Despite the nation's identity as sexually progressive and permissive, sexuality and sensuality are—or were in the 1990s at least—oddly 'passionless' publicly in Aotearoa/New Zealand (see McLauchlan 2012 for a broader discussion of passionlessness in Aotearoa/New Zealand). Alongside this generally muted and 'private' approach to sexuality, public spaces have been strongly marked as heterosexual so expressions of queerness in public spaces have tended to be framed as 'invasion' (Brickell 2000). Although legislation and public attitudes in Aotearoa/New Zealand are increasingly queer-friendly, in the 1990s, echoes of early settler intolerance of gender ambiguity and homosexuality (Coleborne 2014, 473; Povinelli 1994) were still widespread. Yet, as several of the stories— especially 'A quiet story'—attempt to tell, neither homosexuality nor gender queerness were entirely impossible to live out. Alongside strong taboos against men's intimacy with other men and the almost complete invisibility of lesbians, our local bookshop was run by men who lived

---

2   By way of explanation of the sometimes stark difference between representation and reality, as labour historian Melanie Nolan has noted, the settlement of Aotearoa/New Zealand was paired with a powerful history of advertising. More geographically distant from desired Western European migrants than 'competing' settler states such as Canada or Australia, it seems that alluring stories of a land characterised by harmony, prosperity and equality were necessary to encourage people to travel the additional distance to the isolated nation (Nolan 2007). The advertisements, first told in print and later in film, were also communicated at home, seemingly also influencing the self-concept of people from Aotearoa/New Zealand (Nolan 2007), such as myself. The necessity to believe the truth of such advertising—and the taboo against speaking or at times even seeing less-positive realities (see, e.g. Hatch 1991)—may be linked to both the sacrifices made for such migration, as well as the impossibility of returning to 'home' for many migrants, rendering disappointing realities too painful to bear (King 2013). Traditions of 'good advertising' continue and, more recently, can be seen in the ways that pollution and DDT use in farmlands have been overlooked in both tourism advertising and the national self-concept of Aotearoa/New Zealand as '100% Pure' (Bell 1996).

quietly as a couple, and the unabashedly queer Topp Twins, and South Canterbury's own Mika X, were widely celebrated. What is it that makes it sometimes possible to smuggle queerness, whether of sexual orientation, gender identity or both, into worlds that can be violently heteronormative? The charisma of spirits of queer smuggling seemed to be frequently aligned with the more-than-human world (with both gentle-men and butch-leaning women often being respected for their skills in the natural world, whether as hunters or fishers or bush walkers). Yet, the breezes and shimmer of charisma that allow for such possibilities of queer existence— even, at times, celebration—are not entirely reliable, neither in the stories, nor the worlds, they reflect. Yet, they show the possibility of people who are outside of norms being cast as something other than negatively monstrous. In dialogue with queer theory's own long preoccupation with the monstrous (MacCormack 2012), this collection includes at times the cautious yet heartfelt celebration of the shimmer of 'monstrous' traits— often traits with a cross-gender quality.

Running through the collection is also the question of the negotiation of boundaries between human and non-human animals. Growing up in rural New Zealand, bestiality-related insults were at times aimed at boys from my hometown during sporting and other competitions by kids from urban schools. Although we would attempt to hold a united front against the stupidity of 'sheep fucker' taunts, privately at least, some of us held doubts. Rumours about boys (it was only ever boys) from farms having sex with other-than-human animals were a source of occasional yet bewildering horror among small-town girls like myself. Yet, the reality was difficult to discern, as our insight was reliant on boys (particularly those with rural connections) being willing to break rank. I still don't know if or which of such tales were true. Growing up, I knew of just one persistent rumour of a town boy engaging in such behaviour. However, the interspecies transgressions of 'townies' (a term used for those who, like me, didn't live on a farm) tended to be that of emotional incest with 'pets', with too much attachment or 'wasting of money' on extravagant veterinary care on other-than-human animals being a sure-fire way to mark oneself out as a 'townie', with all of the associations of a fundamental lack of commonsense that accompanied that label. While at times funny or silly—with humour being an important aspect of the uncanny (Trnka 2011)—the multispecies uncanny that runs through the category violations of many of these stories is also serious business, often policing gender boundaries with the 'animalising' of those who disobey gender norms and marking important divides not only between rural and urban but also between human (or non-human person) and not. Such life and death boundaries are the animating dynamics in many of the stories, but particularly within 'Claudia the dog' and 'Rabbits etc./placentas'.

Another strand running through the stories are the inequalities of rural pākehā New Zealand—inequalities that exist despite the country's egalitarian reputation. As Elvin Hatch noted in his ethnography of a 1980s South Canterbury town he refers to as 'South Downs', much of life in the region was quietly marked by a desire to be 'respectable' (Hatch 1991). In rural South Canterbury, alongside social sanctions against too directly claiming superior class status, economic class was distinctly enacted, with wealthy rural families dressed in clearly signifying outfits, often including Moleskin trousers, boat shoes, Barker's sweatpants, Aertex shirts and merino jerseys. While some aspects of such clothing have practical applications (with Moleskin trousers, for example, being particularly hardy yet also flexible, or Aertex shirts being breathable), the strongly symbolic nature of such items was clear in the incredulity that would have met a townie wearing them. Wearing such clothing (or not), such as in 'Very pale boy' and 'Indelible couch smell', also signals who is and is not a suitable marriage partner. Yet, a range of portals of connection across differences did exist. Learning to be skilled with one's hands, such as through building, fishing or hunting, or an artistic practice (or to be a child of such people), could allow for some movement (including marital) between urban and rural. Rugby union also allowed for the possibility of warm connections across both class and racialised differences. Unlike in the game's home country, the United Kingdom, rugby union in Aotearoa/New Zealand isn't (just) an upper-class sport. In contrast to much of the rest of the world, soccer is instead the game associated with being middle class, or at least having a first-generation European or British immigrant parent, as is noted in 'Walter Clift'.

A sense of being left behind in class dynamics is a core aspect of the 'dregs' of the title of this collection. Rural primary schools (from the age of five to 10 or 11) are attended by children from a wide range of class backgrounds, from children whose families have faced underemployment and unemployment for several generations to those with inherited farming wealth verging on aristocratic. For the 'intermediate school' years, in which students are aged 10–11 to 11–12, such diversity is often maintained, though in larger groups as rural children are often bused into 'town' to attend the larger combined intermediate and secondary schools that are common in the provincial South Island. From high school age onwards (Form 3/Year 9, age 12–13), however, life becomes more stratified, with many teenagers from middle- and upper-class farming families going to boarding school in Timaru, Christchurch, or Dunedin, for their high school years. Many of the stories of *Dregs*, but most notably 'Indelible couch smell', are set in either the intermediate years in which rural students attend school with 'townies' or those years after many middle- and upper-class rural students have left for more prestigious schooling. It was among these social 'dregs' that I belonged, and among which many of the stories are set.

During the 1990s in which *Dregs* is largely set, South Canterbury, like much of Aotearoa/New Zealand, was in the shadow of 'structural adjustment' introduced in the mid-1980s. The financial distress caused by neoliberal economic reforms and the removal of governmental farming subsidies further increased disparities between rich and poor (Kearns and Joseph 1997; Kelsey 1997; Moran 1999). A sense of distress arising from the economic change and uncertainty of these times is the backdrop to many of the stories. If boundary crossing is associated with the monstrous, I am also interested in the monstrousness that is framed in a heroic light. In my own South Canterbury childhood, neoliberal shifts towards efficiency and productivity were at times lamented as leading to the loss of dignified employment and access to a full host of services. At other times, the willingness to work impossibly hard and to attempt to become more efficient in response to such loss was met with a degree of admiration. Such questions are a core line of inquiry in 'Conjoined butcher minister twins', in which boundaries between human and machinic levels of productivity and discipline are transgressed and elicit complex responses.

Living in the shadows of neoliberal reform meant (and perhaps still does mean) sacrificing human connection in order to face the challenges of maintaining a living. Accompanying such economic 'rationalisation', rural parts of the country faced a more general sense of decline and abandonment. Suicide rates in remote rural districts and those with low urban influence increased sharply in the late 1980s and mid-1990s in New Zealand, to reach twice the national male average by 1999–2001 (Pearce, Barnett and Jones 2007). During my own high school years, at least one boy died every year. Some of the deaths were suicides, others tragic accidents, but we were left with a degree of loss that remains hard to fathom and that I suspect has shaped both my own career and, certainly, this collection of stories. Many of the stories in this collection wrestle with questions of masculine gentleness and feeling, the sweet monstrous other of the 'strong and silent' ideals that retain currency in New Zealand, particularly in the south (Jensen 1996). Urged against by variously misogynist or homophobic cries of 'don't be a girl', or 'don't be sissy', the presence of deep sweetness and the capacity and need for connection among people of all genders, but particularly of boys and men, is an animating aspect of the stories. Despite taboos against masculine tenderness, small yet life-giving transgressions, as traced in the stories of Christopher Martin ('A quiet story') and 'Walter Clift', were, and I believe remain, possible.[3]

Stoicism in Aotearoa is also an aspect of the performance of whiteness; it has become an everyday and under-recognised aspect of the ongoing violence of colonisation (Borell 2021; Hokowhitu 2007). Despite having an

---

3   I would like to extend heart-felt gratitude to Mr Michael Deavoll, who taught art at Geraldine High School. Mr Deavoll was not only a spectacular and encouraging art teacher, but also was deeply skilled in making spaces that could hold both ruggedly outdoorsy and deeply tender masculinities. His art room was a place of sanctuary for me and many other students. Thank you.

international image as an integrated, bicultural nation, ongoing settler colonial dominance means that other lifeways do not exert equal influence. Unlike the majority of Māori who move with skill between te ao Māori and te ao pākeha—that is, between Māori and pākehā worlds—it is rare for pākehā to be similarly aware of or engaged with te ao Māori (Fozdar 2014, 209). Returning to Anzaldúa's work and the richness of 'borderland thinking', in which one is able to hold contradictions and multiple ways of seeing, the largely pākehā and often Protestant views followed in these stories often actively reject such possibilities, with colonial inequalities allowing such worldviews to represent 'the truth'. The possibilities of generative connection outside of white Protestant lifeways are suggested in several of the stories, particularly 'Indelible couch smell' and 'A quiet story'. However, reflecting both the lack of curiosity about other lifeways that being part of a dominant group allows, and the rules of polite engagement typical of 'progressive' pākehā, discussions of ethnic, racialised and religious differences were largely avoided in the worlds in which I grew up. Thus, while I might know that a friend or classmate was not white or of a Protestant background—and that their presence at times afforded some kind of aliveness and possibility that was not part of my inherited worldview—I rarely found out more about what it was that animated them, how they identified or the worlds to which they belonged. The stories reflect this lack of connection and understanding. For those readers who share a similar background to me, I hope that attending to the bleakness of such a way of moving in the world might help to encourage us towards other, more generative, ways of being and relating.

Social monsters

Monsters, I believe, can be generative forces. I first met the term 'monstrous feminine' through spending time with Master of Screen Production students at the University of Auckland,[4] among whom Barbara Creed's term the 'monstrous feminine' had a great deal of currency.[5] I was encouraged to think with such forces particularly by Lisa Samuels as part of the Master of Creative Writing program at the University of Auckland at which this collection first emerged.[6] As Creed (1993) notes, the same tendency to see aspects of the feminine as monstrous also reads the presence of the feminine in bodies identified as male as a monstrous lack. Through both the initial writing of this collection, as well as the process of re-editing some 13 years later, I've come to take the monstrous feminine

---

4   A shout out to Paul Veart, who has been integral to the entirety of this collection, as well as to Jennifer Garcia, Maria Zagoreos and Sara Root.
5   While my mother also happens to be named Barbara Creed, this Barbara Creed is (I believe) not my mother. A shout-out to both Barbara Creeds.
6   I particularly thank Lisa for asking me what has come to strike me as a question of feminist solidarity and encouragement: 'what do you care about?' And, when I answered, 'the monstrous feminine', for urging me to write about that with unruly grammar.

deeply seriously, regardless of the gender identity of the person from whom it emerges. And I wonder what gold—even the gold of potential flourishing of humans and land—there might be in such denied shadows. In telling stories of the monstrous feminine, I hope to participate in the anthropological tradition of offering moments of generativity and glimpses of possibilities otherwise (Robbins 2013; Pandian 2019).

Monsters to live well alongside are in no shortage in other parts of Aotearoa/New Zealand. Other collections told by other tellers in other parts of the country would look remarkably different and, indeed, could tell of a host of generative boundary-transgressing creatures actively animating the world. The entities of Māori worlds—such as taniwha living in waterways, the guardians of the pounamu after which Te Waipounamu (the South Island) is named; the manaia guardians moving between spirit and human worlds; the patupaiarehe, the fairy-like beings living in the mists of mountain tops and forest—were not typically acknowledged as beings or forces with which to attempt to live well in the pākehā world of my childhood. When translated into my pākehā world, stories of such beings became myths and tales rather than lore and guides to cohabitation with creatures or forces requiring respect.

It is not that my own ancestors—or those of other pākehā—lacked monsters. I had adored European folktales about witches and helpful animals, changelings and selkies. Yet they somehow they didn't seem *alive*— at least in my readings of such stories while dwelling on South Canterbury lands. They remained stories. Such relegation of monsters to the fictional, Musharbash argues, is also tied to cultural shifts in Western Europe, from 'the Renaissance and the Reformation, through the Enlightenment and Scientific Revolution' (Musharbash 2014, 4). Yet alongside this dismissal, the killing of people as witches begins *after* the Reformation. Aspects of the monstrous retain this twin tone of being both fictional and yet needing to be erased. With the dominance of Protestant Christianity in the regions that grew me up, suspicion of anything that might look like 'papism'[7] also ensured there was little possibility of relating to otherly forces, not for exorcism, let alone adorcism—the possibility of having an ongoing relationship with the entity (Csordas 2019). Historian Jock Phillips also suggests that Protestant, more than Catholic, settlers also had a tendency towards a lack of connection to the past, leading the majority Protestant settler colony to have a particularly strong 'collective amnesia', a forgetting of ancestors and roots (Phillips 2013). In this climate, the overly religious, or even having faith in anything outside of the strictly 'rational', can take on a forbidden monstrous sheen.

---

7   While supposedly non-sectarian, other scholars have noted the quiet, anti-Catholic sentiment underlying dominant culture in Aotearoa/New Zealand (see Jones 2020).

The existing world of monsters into which those of *Dregs* enter is thus limited. A biographical figure had stood in for the monstrous for many South Islanders, particularly for those from the 'deep South' of the South Island. Minnie Dean, a working-class pākehā woman who made her living taking in babies of unmarried mothers, was tried and convicted of infanticide following the death of six of the 28 children she claimed to have cared for. She was hanged in Invercargill in 1895. The only woman to face the death penalty in New Zealand, Dean, in her spectral afterlife, was evoked as a threat to unruly children, particularly in the South Island. By the time of my childhood in the 1990s, however, even her power seemed to be waning, and the threat of 'Minnie Dean will get you' was rarely uttered, particularly so far north as South Canterbury.

Recent times have seen the growth of more monsters: the early career films of Peter Jackson, such as *The Valley* (1976), *Bad Taste* (1987) and *Meet the Feebles* (1989), told the tales of local monsters, while *Heavenly Creatures* (1994) and *Forgotten Silver* (1995) told stories of 'real' characters—the 1950s Christchurch-based teen murderers Pauline Parker and Juliet Hulme, and South Canterbury's own reclusive inventor Richard Pierce—a figure who, to my mind, carries a socially sanctioned shimmer of the monstrous feminine. Films by other directors, including Jonathan King's *Black Sheep* (2006) and Taika Waititi's *What We Do in the Shadows* (2014), have also explored the possibilities of monsters in our midst. Perhaps living well with monsters in worlds descended from Enlightenment views means our monsters will have literary aspects. However, I am hoping for a possibility of approaching such creatures as being more than literary, of being, instead, shadowy forces to live with and, perhaps, with gifts that might finally be accepted.

The monstrous, this collection affirms, is in many ways inevitable. If some structures and boundaries are part of all lifeways, surely there will always be beings who transgress them. To live with such others without an idea of who they are or how one might best show respect feels like a risky— or at least depleted—business. Writing towards an anthropology of the unspeakable, Dragojilovic and Samuels (2021, 417) argue that 'silence can be a haunting or lingering ghost from the past that is uncannily present in the narratives and modes of life that constitute people's imaginative possibilities and horizons of expectation'. *Dregs* is my attempt to offer an— albeit limited and particular—name for several such haunting presences in the hope of entering into generative relations with them. These stories are thus offered in the hope that other voices with different knowings will join mine, helping to do the work of meeting—or even befriending—our own ghosts, so that we might have the possibility of smiling at the strange, both inside and out (Kristeva 1991, 191).

Laura McLauchlan
December 2024

References

Anzaldúa, Gloria. 1999. *Borderlands/La Frontera*. San Francisco: Aunt Lute Books.

Bell, Claudia. 1996. *Inventing New Zealand: Everyday Myths of Pakeha Identity*. Auckland: Penguin Books.

Borell, Belinda. 2021. 'The Role of Emotion in Understanding Whiteness'. *Journal of Bioethical Inquiry* 18 (1): 23–31. doi.org/10.1007/s11673-020-10074-z.

Brickell, Chris. 2000. 'Heroes and Invaders: Gaylene and Lesbian Pride Parades and the Public/Private Distinction in New Zealand Media Accounts'. *Gender, Place & Culture* 7 (2): 163–78. doi.org/10.1080/713668868.

Clifford, James. 1983. 'On Ethnographic Authority'. *Representations* 1 (2): 118–46. doi.org/10.2307/2928386.

Clifford, James. 1986. 'Introduction: Partial Truths'. In *Writing Culture: The Poetics and Politics of Ethnography*, edited by James Clifford and George Marcus, 1–26. Berkeley: University of California Press.

Coleborne, Catherine. 2014. 'White Men and Weak Masculinity: Men in the Public Asylums in Victoria, Australia, and New Zealand, 1860s–1900s'. *History of Psychiatry* 25 (4): 468–76. doi.org/10.1177/0957154X14543758.

Creed, Barbara. 1993. *The Monstrous-Feminine: Film, Feminism, Psychoanalysis*. London: Routledge.

Csordas, Thomas J. 2019. 'Specter, Phantom, Demon'. *Ethos* 47 (4): 519–29. doi.org/10.1111/etho.12253.

Dragojlovic, Ana and Annemarie Samuels. 2021. 'Tracing Silences: Towards an Anthropology of the Unspoken and Unspeakable'. *History and Anthropology* 32 (4): 417–25. doi.org/10.1080/02757206.2021.1954634.

Fairburn, Miles. 2013. *The Ideal Society and its Enemies: The Foundations of Modern New Zealand Society*. Auckland: Auckland University Press.

Fozdar, Farida. 2014. 'Among Friends? On the Dynamics of Maori–Pakeha Relationships in Aotearoa New Zealand'. *New Zealand Sociology* 29 (1): 206–10.

Francis, H. T. (trans.). 1897. '432: Padakusalamāṇava-jātaka'. In *The Jātaka or Stories of the Buddha's Former Births. Volume III*, edited by E. B. Cowell, 298–306. Cambridge: Cambridge University Press.

Giblett, Rod. 2008. 'Monstrous Body of the Slimy Depths'. In *The Body of Nature and Culture*, 74–89. London: Palgrave Macmillan.

Haraway, Donna. 1988. 'Situated Knowledges: The Science Question in Feminism and the Privilege of Partial Perspective'. *Feminist Studies* 14 (3): 575–99. doi.org/10.2307/3178066.

Hatch, Elvin. 1991. *Respectable Lives: Social Standing in Rural New Zealand*. California: University of California Press. doi.org/10.1525/california/9780520074729.001. 0001.

Hayes, Barbara. 1987. *Folk Tales And Fables of The World*. New York: Barnes and Noble.

Hokowhitu, Brendan. 2007. 'The Silencing of Māori Men'. *New Zealand Journal of Counselling* 27 (2): 63–76.

Jensen, K. 1996. *Whole Men: The Masculine Tradition in New Zealand Literature*. Auckland: Auckland University Press.

Jones, Alison. 2020. *This Pākehā Life: An Unsettled Memoir*. Wellington: Bridget Williams Books.

Kearns, Robin A. and Alun E. Joseph. 1997. 'Restructuring Health and Rural Communities in New Zealand'. *Progress in Human Geography* 21 (1): 18–32.

Kelsey, Jane. 1997. 'Employment and Union Issues in New Zealand-12 Years on'. *California Western International Law Journal* 28 (1): 253.

King, Michael. 2013. *Being Pakeha Now*. Auckland: Penguin Random House New Zealand.

Kristeva, Julia. 1991. *Strangers to Ourselves*. New York: Columbia University Press.

Laterza, V. 2007. 'The Ethnographic Novel'. *Suomen Antropologi: Journal of the Finnish Anthropological Society* 32 (2): 124–34.

Lyons, Thomas .2003. 'The Ethnographic Novel and Ethnography in Colonial Algeria'. *Modern Philology* 100 (4): 576–95. doi.org/10.1086/379984.

MacCormack, Patricia. 2012. 'The Queer Ethics of Monstrosity'. In *Speaking of Monsters: A Teratological Anthology*, edited by Caroline Joan S. Picart and John Edgar Browning, 255–65. New York: Palgrave Macmillan. doi.org/10.1057/ 9781137101495_23.

Marcus, George E. and Dick Cushman. 1982. 'Ethnographies as Texts'. *Annual Review of Anthropology* 11: 25–69. doi.org/10.1146/annurev.an.11.100182.000325.

McLauchlan, Gordon. 2012. *The Passionless People Revisited*. New Zealand: David Bateman.

McLauchlan, L. 2024. *Hedgehogs, Killing, and Kindness: The Contradictions of Care in Conservation Practice*. Cambridge: MIT Press.

Moran, Warren. 1999. 'Democracy and Geography in the Reregulation of New Zealand'. In *Restructuring Societies: Insights from the Social Sciences*, edited by D.B. Knight and A.E. Joseph, 33–58. Montreal: McGill-Queen's University Press. doi.org/10.1515/9780773574151-006.

Musharbash, Yasmine. 2014. 'Introduction: Monsters, Anthropology, and Monster Studies'. In *Monster Anthropology in Australasia and beyond*, edited by Yasmine Musharbash and Geir Henning Presterudstuen, 1–24. New York: Palgrave Macmillan. doi.org/10.1057/9781137448651_1.

Musharbash, Yasmine. 2023 [2021]. 'Monsters'. In *The Open Encyclopedia of Anthropology*, edited by Felix Stein. Facsimile of the first edition in *The Cambridge Encyclopedia of Anthropology*. doi.org/10.29164/21monsters.

Narayan, Kirin. 1999. 'Ethnography and Fiction: Where Is the Border?' *Anthropology and Humanism* 24 (2): 134–47. doi.org/10.1525/ahu.1999.24.2.134.

Nolan, Melanie. 2007. 'The Reality and Myth of New Zealand Egalitarianism: Explaining the Pattern of a Labour Historiography at the Edge of Empires'. *Labour History Review* 72 (2). doi.org/10.1179/174581807X224560.

Pandian, Anand. 2019. *A Possible Anthropology: Methods for Uneasy Times*. Durham and London: Duke University Press. doi.org/10.1215/9781478004370.

Pearce, Jamie, Ross Barnett and Irfon Jones. 2007. 'Have Urban/Rural Inequalities in Suicide in New Zealand Grown during the Period 1980–2001?' *Social Science & Medicine* 65 (8): 1807–19. doi.org/10.1016/j.socscimed.2007.05.044.

Phillips, Jock. 2013. *Settlers: New Zealand Immigrants from England, Ireland and Scotland 1800–1945*. Auckland: Auckland University Press.

Povinelli, Elizabeth A. 1994. 'Sexual Savages/Sexual Sovereignty: Australian Colonial Texts and the Postcolonial Politics of Nationalism'. *Diacritics* 24 (2/3): 122–50. doi.org/10.2307/465168.

Robbins, Joel. 2013. 'Beyond the Suffering Subject: Toward an Anthropology of the Good'. *Journal of the Royal Anthropological Institute* 19 (3): 447–62. doi.org/10.1111/1467-9655.12044.

Sarukkai, Sundar. 1997. 'The "Other" in Anthropology and Philosophy'. *Economic and Political Weekly* 32 (24): 1406–09.

Schmidt, Nancy J. 1984. 'Ethnographic Fiction: Anthropology's Hidden Literary Style'. *Anthropology and Humanism Quarterly* 9 (4): 11–14. doi.org/10.1525/ahu.1984.9.4.11.

Smith, Linda Tuhiwai, Graham H. Smith, Megan Boler, Margaret Kempton, Adreanne Ormond, Ho- Chia Chueh and Rona Waetford. 2002. '"Do You Guys Hate Aucklanders Too?" Youth: Voicing Difference from the Rural Heartland'. *Journal of Rural Studies* 18 (2): 169–78. doi.org/10.1016/S0743-0167(01)00037-7.

Synnott, Anthony. 1991. 'A Sociology of Smell'. *Canadian Review of Sociology/Revue canadienne de sociologie* 28 (4): 437–9. doi.org/10.1111/j.1755-618X.1991.tb00164.x.

Trnka, Susanna. 2011. 'Specters of Uncertainty: Violence, Humour, and the Uncanny in Indo-Fijian Communities Following the May 2000 Fiji Coup'. *Ethos* 39 (3): 331–48. doi.org/10.1111/j.1548-1352.2011.01196.x.

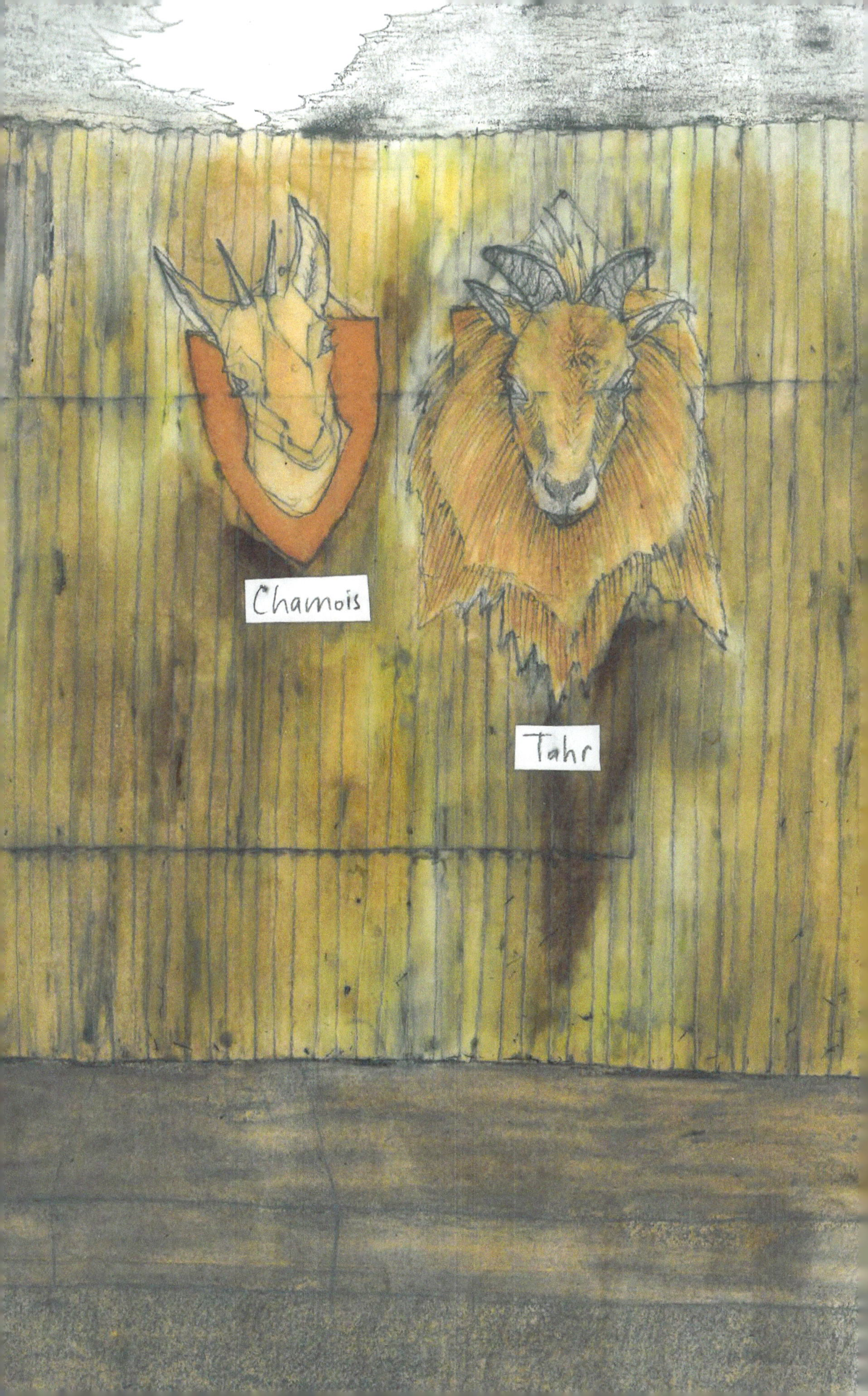

Chamois
Tahr

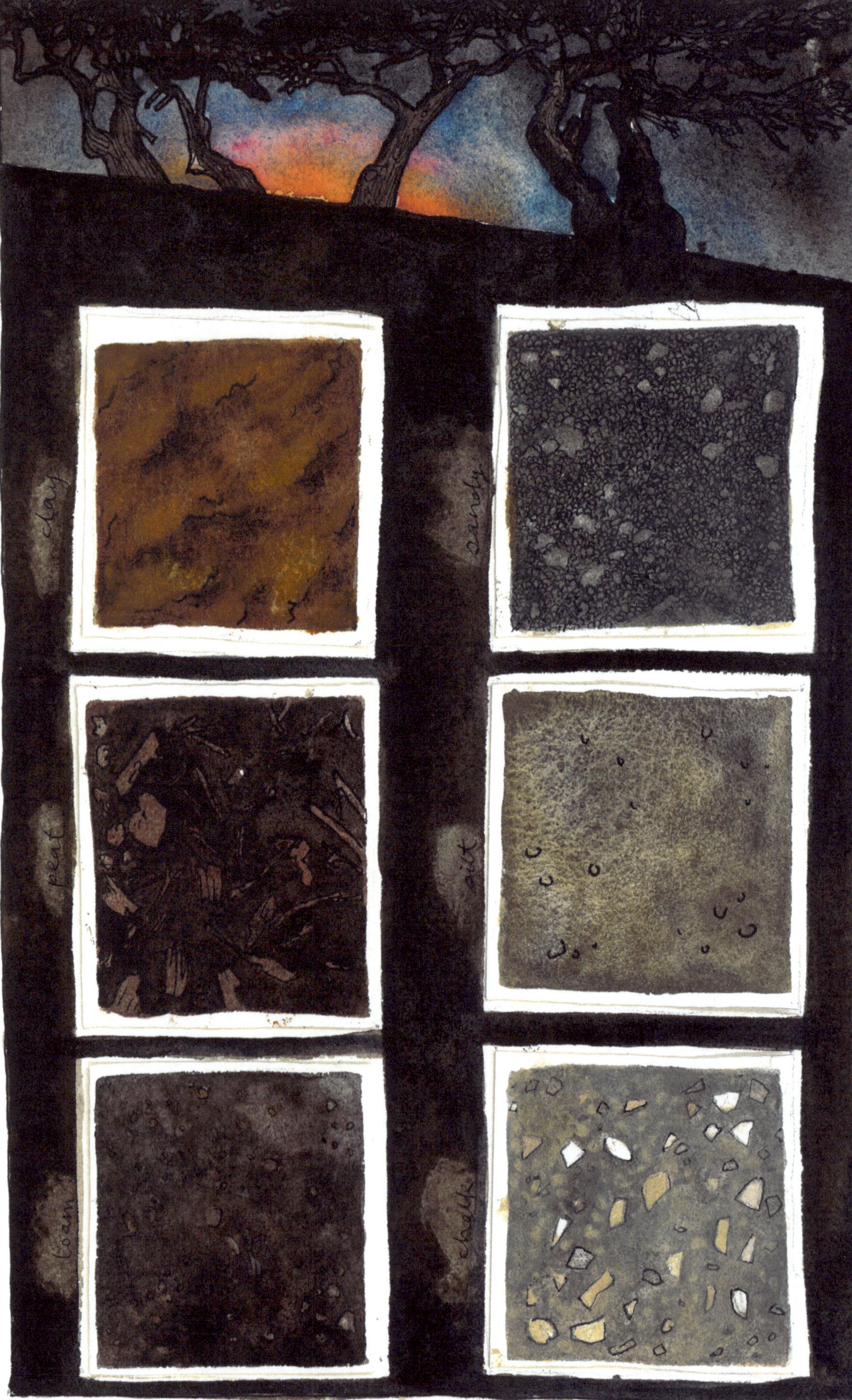
clay
sandy
peat
silt
loam
chalky

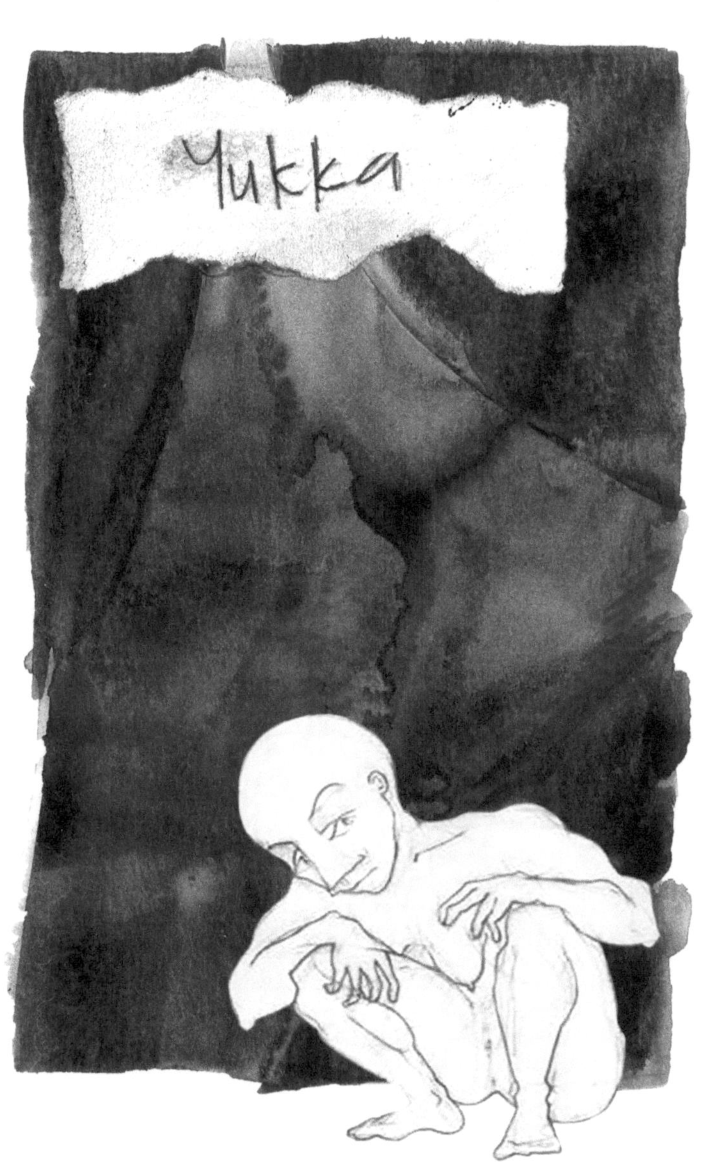
Yukka

East of Dregs, more than 10 farms past the McKerchers' paddocks, but not quite so far as the foot alps, the Edgelands present a warm bush opening through which hunters crawl in the May–June rut after chamois and tahr. When Yukka lived there, huge and strong with an oddly shaped head, some hunters didn't come back. No-one ever saw remains, so no-one could be sure, but word spread that Yukka could bite through bone and had eaten their carcasses whole. Some men still hunted regardless and each year some didn't come home. Townsfolk nodded to those who came back but never asked about what they had seen, the past sometimes better left there.

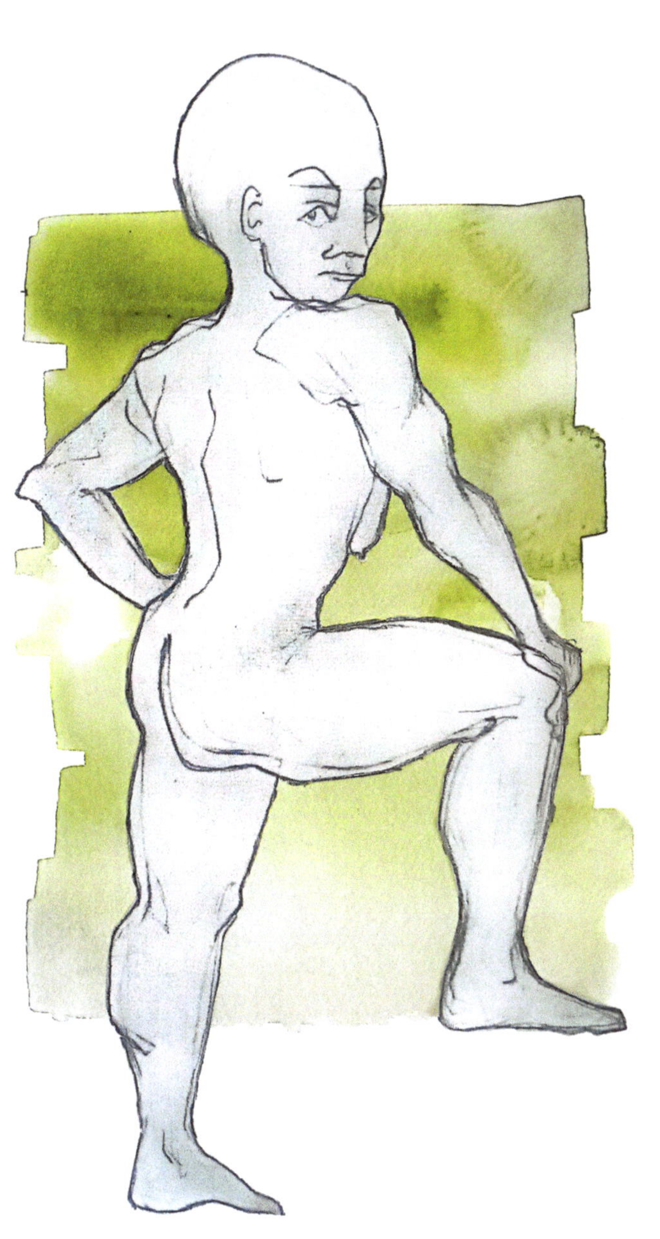

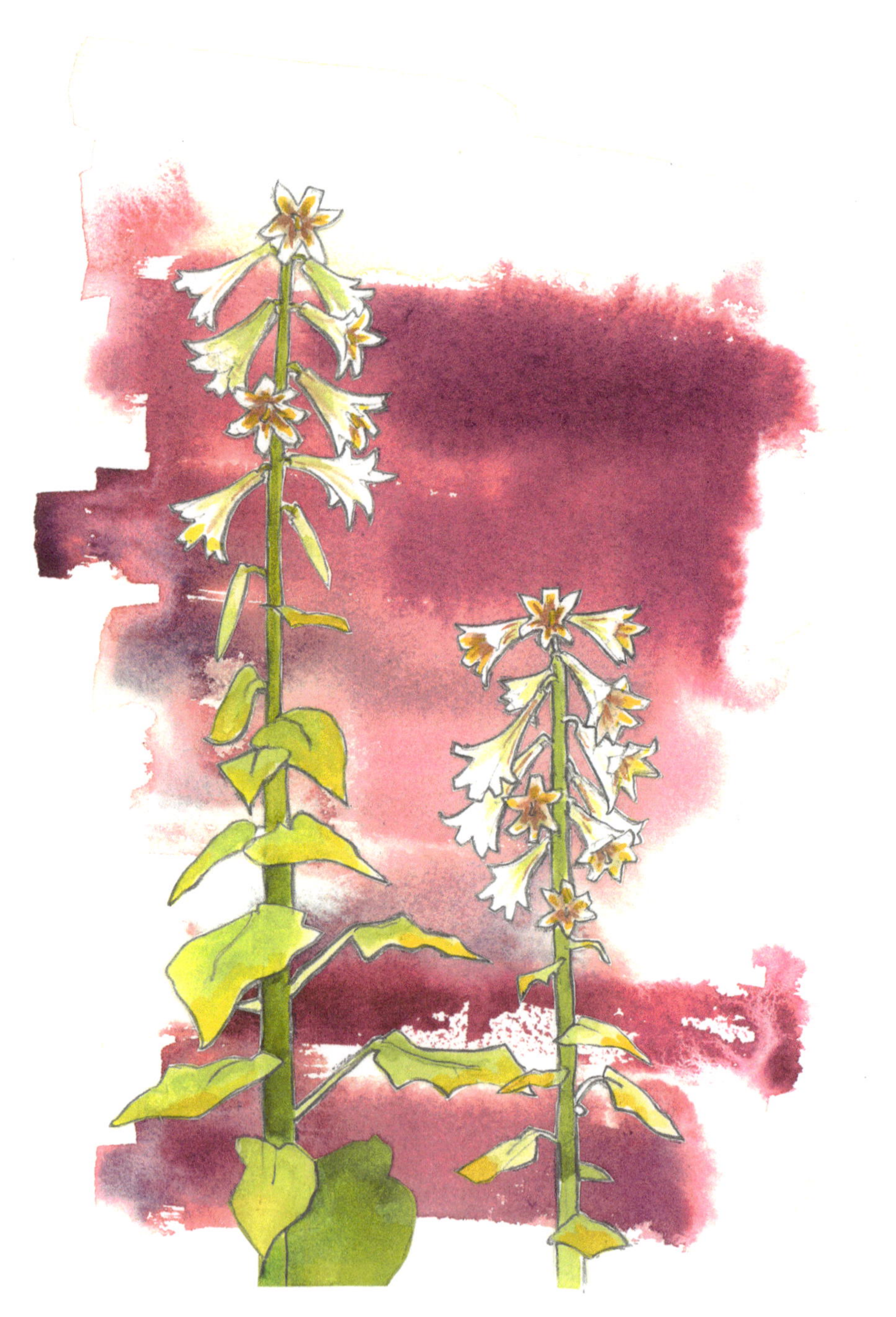

The young deacon of St Martha's Anglican had been bedridden when he was young, missing many things from boot-tying to training dogs and rifles, so he'd never been up to the Edgelands. He had bloomed late and, some thought, unimpressively. But not young Gretchen Stewart, who quite admired his lanky frame. And, as it turned out, not Yukka.

The deacon's leanness was not from hardness, but from a persistent eating from his insides. Even back then, when Dregs still had two town doctors, and both had searched and searched for the root of it, neither had found a thing. But Mrs Grosvenor had named it a spiritual malady one Michaelmas when she'd watched him shiver through the whole of the organ voluntary. Her naming of it stuck and the self-consumptive was offered the deaconship in the hope that the responsibility might prove heartening. A new deacon had been needed, anyway.

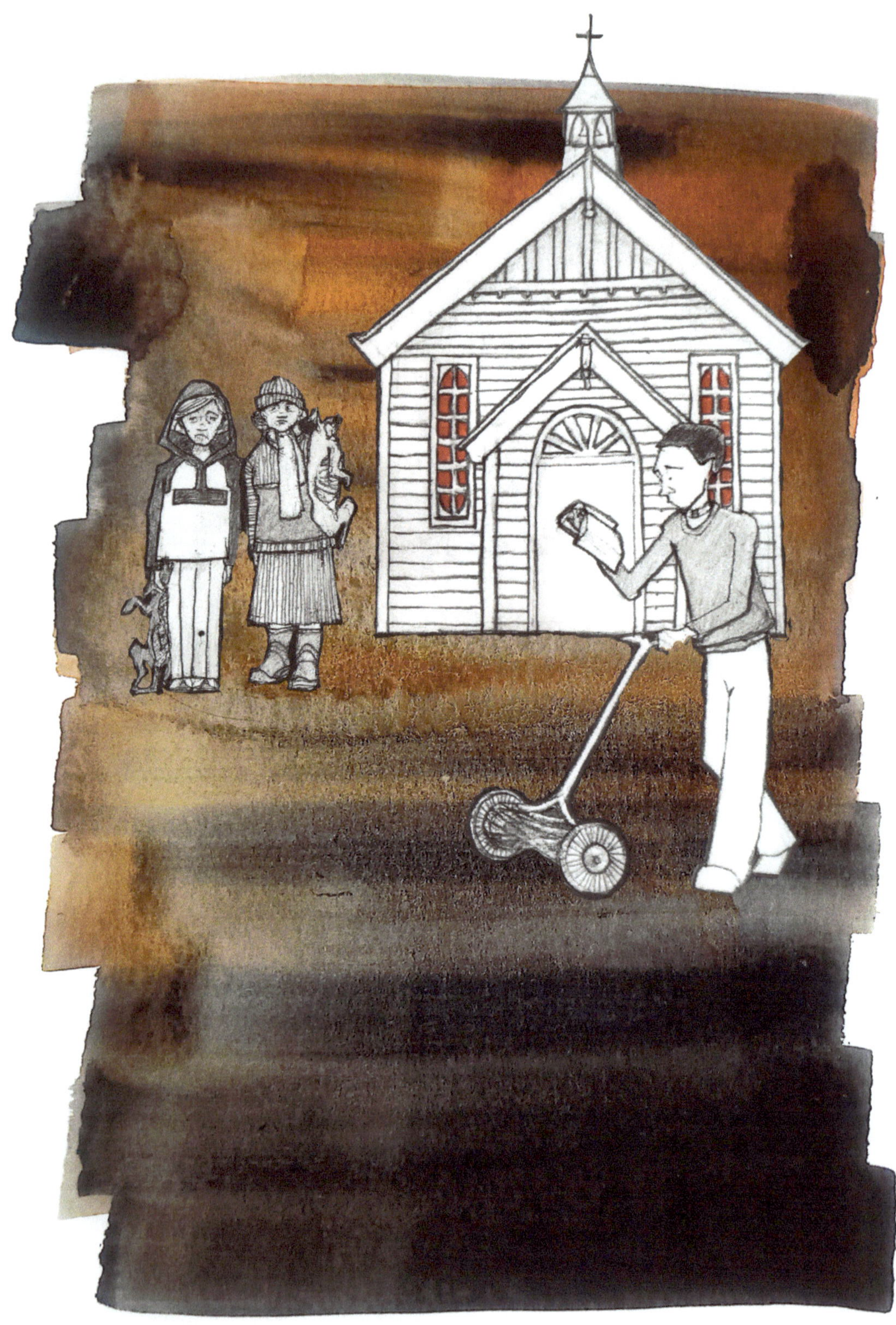

Though the boys in town laughed at the deacon for being so serious in a role last held by Joseph Meek's almost-mute aunt, colour arrived in his cheeks. He mediated in tea committee disputes and mowed the lawns with real feeling. Not a practical man, but conscientious, he mowed even after it rained, and patches of bog formed in the churchyard. But mostly there were missing hunters to process where, in the absence of bodies, there were clothes to lay out and speak of and bury. The deacon tended the wives as they mourned, and assisted the vicar as they married again, this time to out-of-towners with hard, round bellies and ever-gleaming utes. Later, the women would visit his office and confess to lost-husband dreams. The deacon raised plaques to hunters in the vestibule and referred to the men in honorifics until people whispered of a papist tone to his speech, and the JP suggested he stop.

In his third year, the church lawns turned to mud, and still more hunters didn't return—even Peter Owens, who had been famous for caution. What is she? Other troubled creatures had tired and died in due course, but it seemed she just lived on. The wives pestered the deacon, as a man of the cloth, to go up and find out. He figured to go in the sunlight and climbed up to the loamy Edgelands one morning after he'd washed.

Yukka slept during the day in a thick-smelling cave littered with marrow-sucked bones. But, even sleeping, she smelled the deacon's full-grown Protestant scent—a salt and anxious clean sweat—and found herself keenly awake. She moved down the Edgelands to find the smell's source.

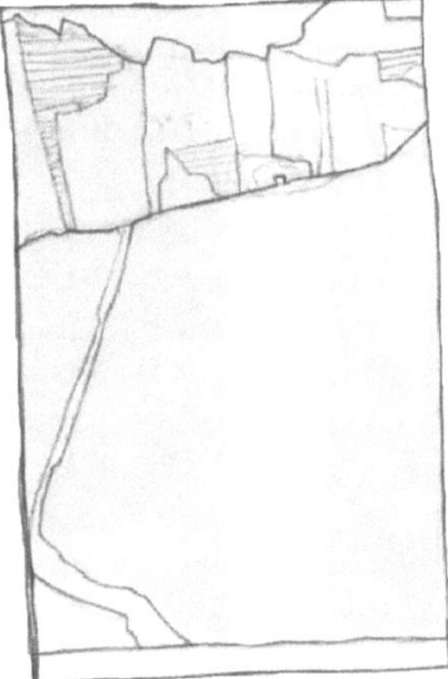

She crept very close to the deacon and smelled the trace of old sickness under the folds of his clothes. A smell that promised rot-hollowed holes. Yukka made plans for her nests in those gaps.

But where might I enter him? She wondered.

Yukka reached for the deacon. His fear smelled high and attractive.

And she offered him a choice:
I eat you, or we wed.

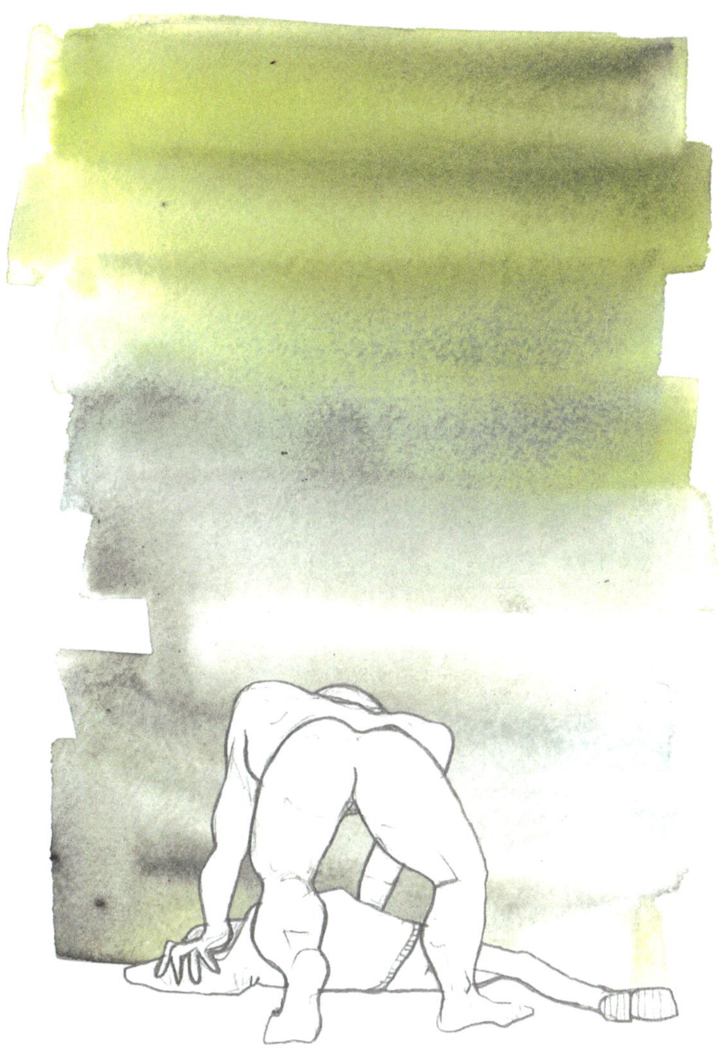

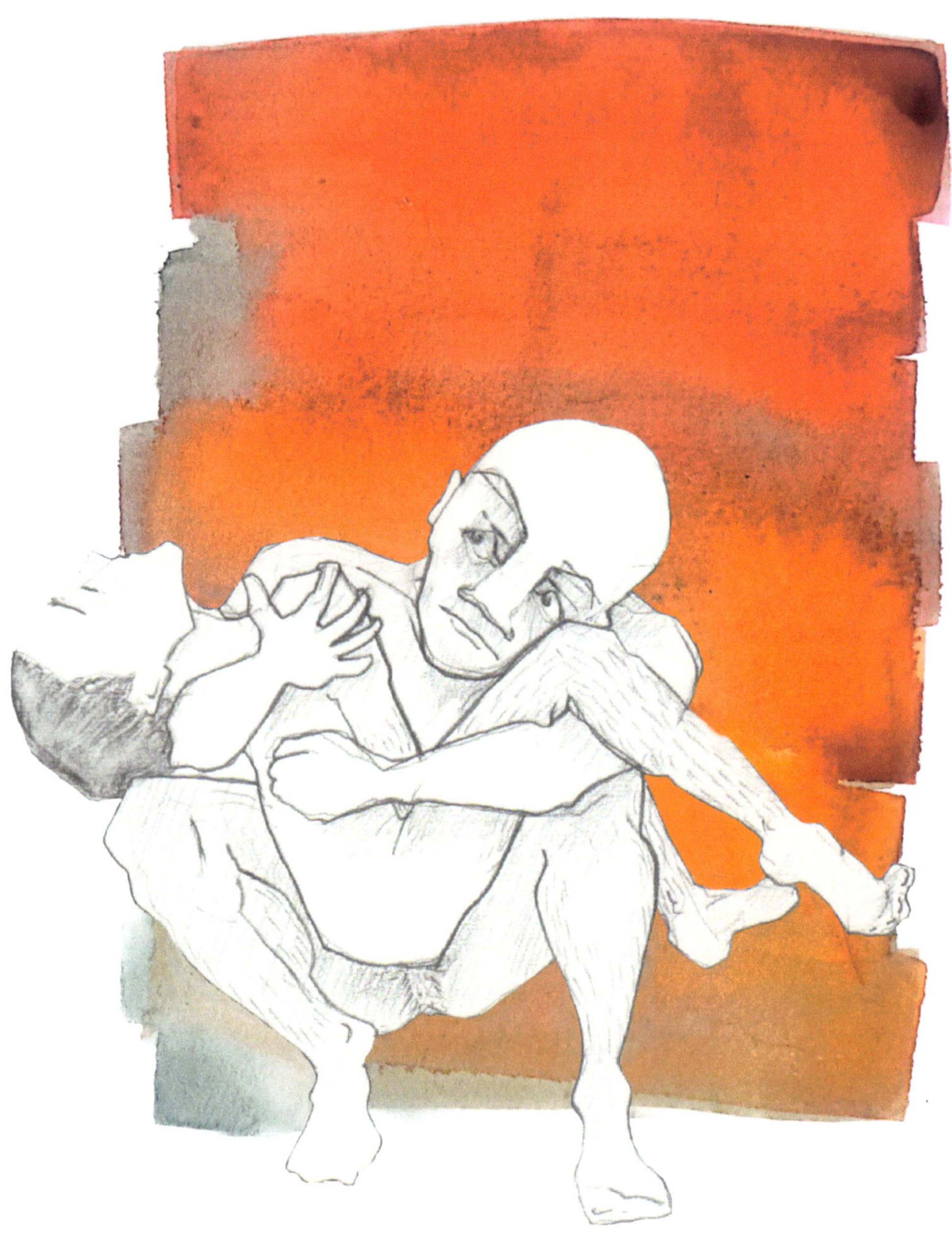

The wedding was small

and smelled
heavy.

She took the deacon back to her cave and heaved
a boulder over the entrance behind them.

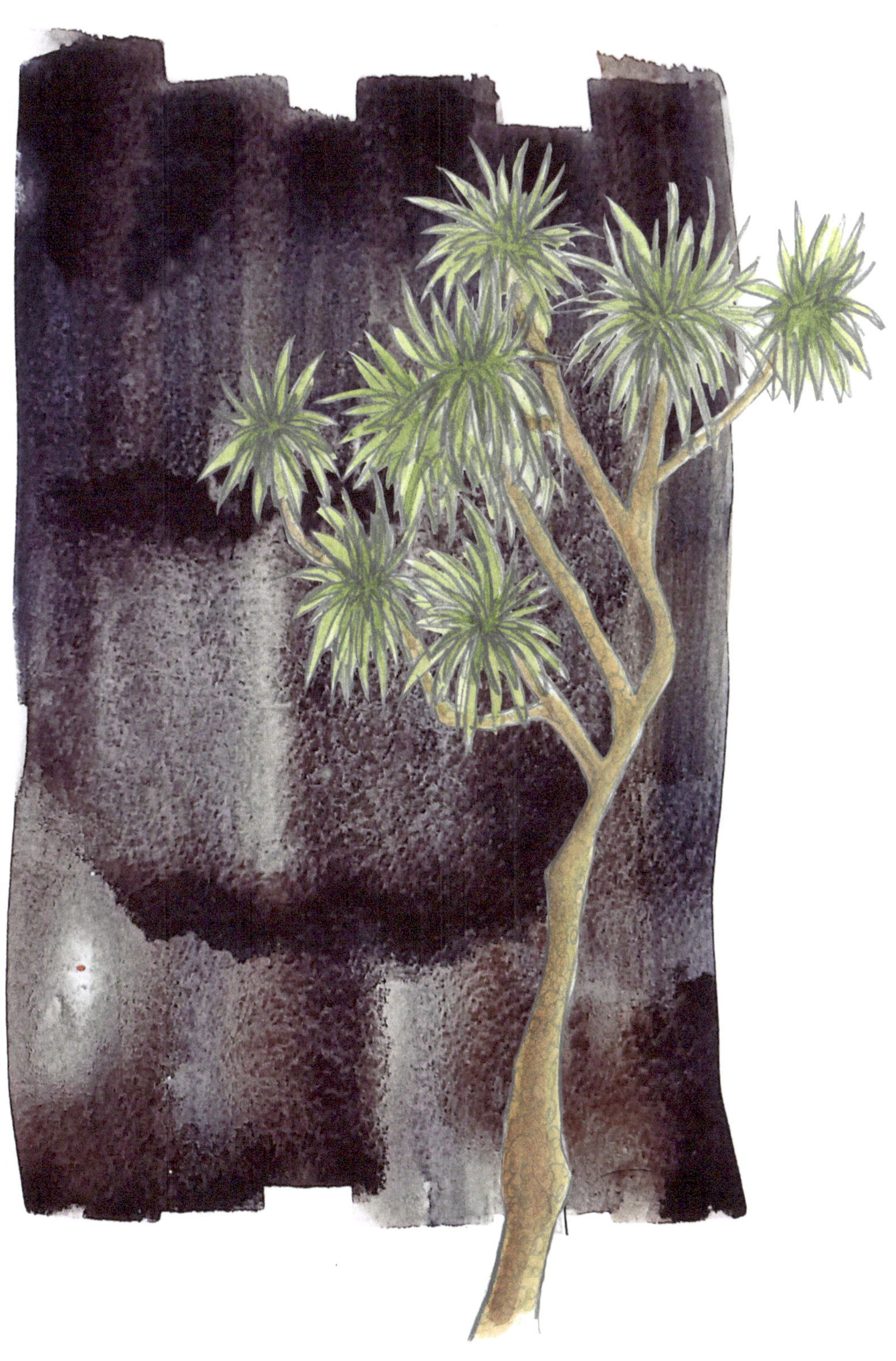

Well before light, Yukka left the cave to hunt, shunting the boulder back in place as she left. The deacon shivered in the dank. Just on dawn, she returned, gentle sun reaching into the cave as she rolled back the boulder and hauled in a fresh bloody thar. The deacon shat, and she stroked him. She ripped a leg from the tahr, and he shook as she growled at him to eat. She smelled his food as it travelled through his insides and wondered at how little he pulled from it.

With his back turned and quivering, the deacon scratched Michael, Gabriel, and Raphael into the rock and waited to see if anyone would reply, but none did. He carved Uriel in deeper and then Christopher, and Christopher told him to run, so he ran, but he was slow on his rot-weakened legs. Yukka caught him in a stride and pinned him, and bit through his thigh as he cried.

In the cave, Yukka licked at her husband's great wound.

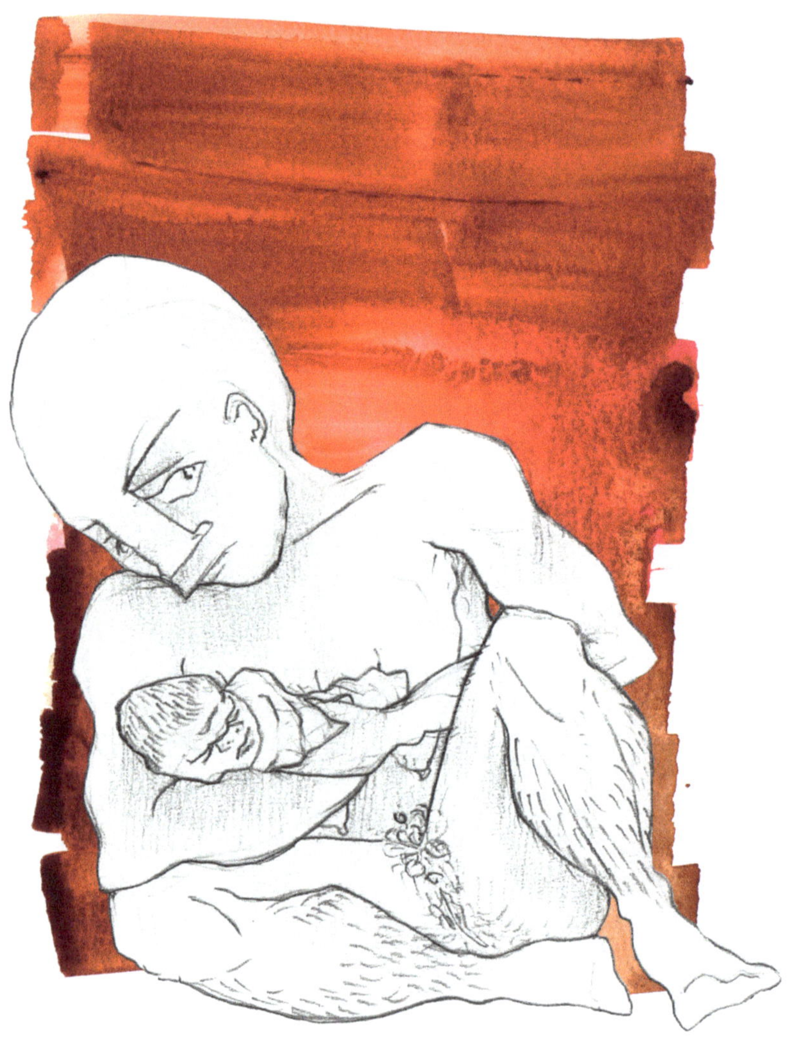

A baby came.

The baby's cries carried, and the township couldn't help but imagine the woe of the deacon. His woe.

Poor our deacon, the folk of St Martha's said, he is lost to us in the Edgelands. First Presbyterian added his name to Sunday Community Thoughts and the Methodists suggested a vigil with candles in the Village Green to be held all together. And so, for the first time in Dregs, the Protestant three let bygones be gone and prayed together against a far greater threat. And at Guy Fawkes they agreed not to light crackers and, in a gesture to even the folks of St Patrick's, they removed the papal coat of arms from around the Guy's neck, and it never went back on again.

But, quietly, excitement mixed with the worry in Dregs and required firm holding down. People dreamed of sinkhole pools rising up and liming their land and of pukeko and cows laying tits up in the sun. They woke flustered; husbands and wives averting eyes from one another, they grounded themselves by speaking their chore lists aloud and through regular grain-based breakfasts—a cold-breakfast habit that would return again every spring.

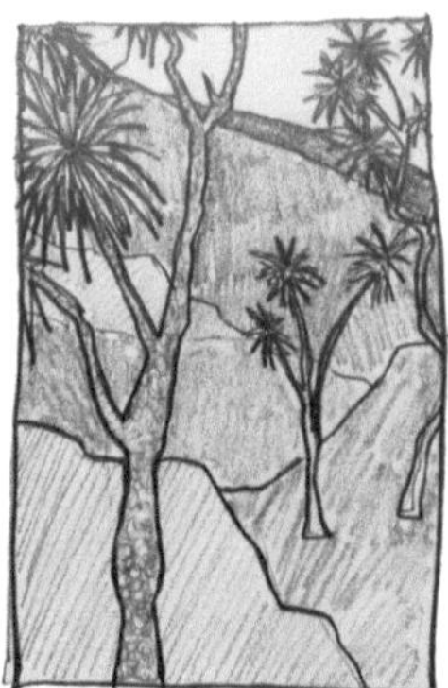

Each day up in the Edgelands things went on much as they had, but with the couple now a three. The deacon still wrote in the ground, but carefully now, never Christopher, the scar on his leg throbbing at the sight of a travelling saint. Each dawn, when Yukka returned she opened the cave and kept it so for a time, smelling her baby's love of the light. The deacon scrawled thanks in the soil for the sun. And, as he did, he marvelled at the sweet dark loam in his fingers. He'd never noticed how beautiful soil could be.

With father and son returned to the cave as Yukka slept, the boy, even as a babe, followed the sun as it moved through the gaps between boulder and wall, crawling then walking from light beam to beam. As the boy followed the patches of sun, his father told stories of life he'd heard as a deacon down there in the light, tales of drapers and shelving and competitive paddock fencing that the boy asked to hear over and over.

One morning in autumn, as they all ate in the thin morning sun, Yukka smelled at her boy as he chewed, his bones straining towards the weak orange-red light, pulling what he could of it into his marrow. By the end of the meal, with her son's stomach full but his bones hardly done, it pained her to pull him back in the dark. So she left the boy with her husband in front of the cave into the sun for the day. Out to grow in the light while she slept in the cave.

She would call them back in at night.

Stay. And they did.

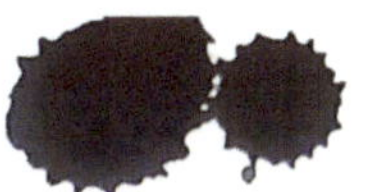
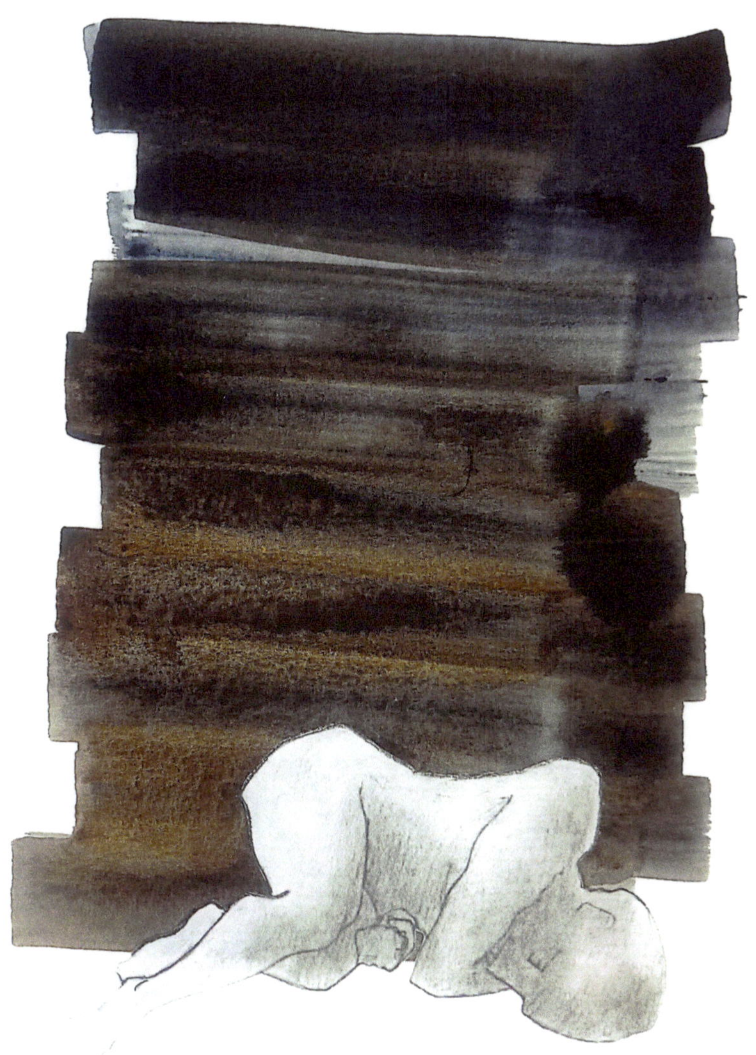

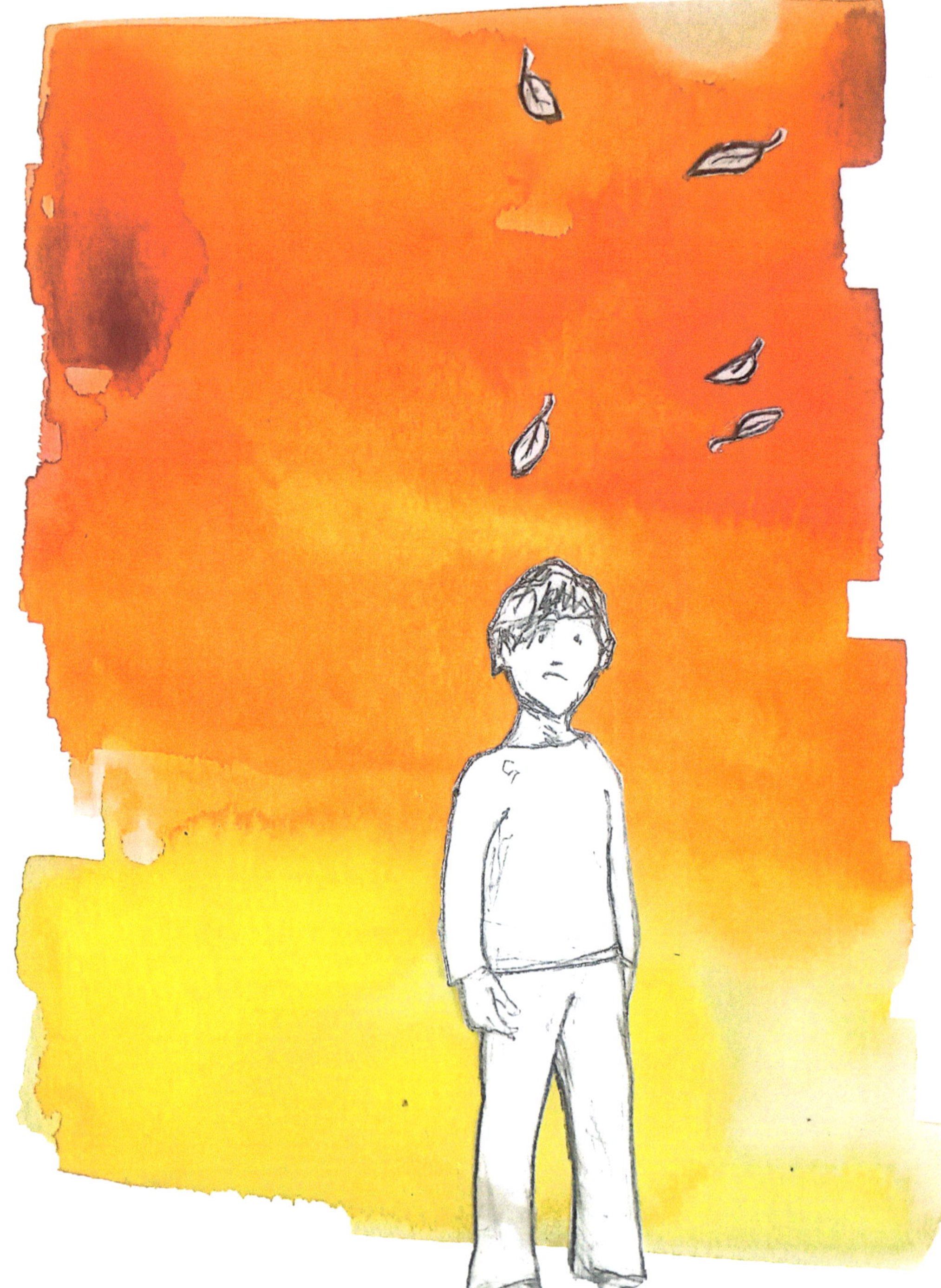

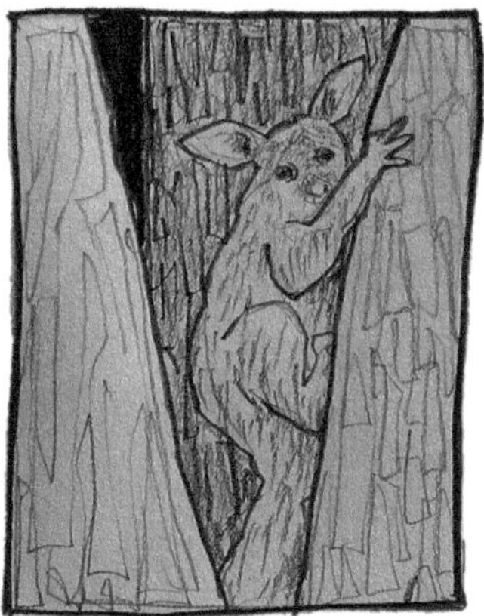

So days passed with goat and thar and chamois, autumn into winter sun, nights warm in the cave. In spring, the deacon's hands calm in the warming soil, not just writing but growing, planting from seeds Yukka brought back from the hunt so that the cave was surrounded by blackberries and carrots and even a wild crop of parsley. And the boy grew in what seemed triple time in the months and months that passed, growing with the strength of his mother, but more the look of his dad.

When the summer days got so that wearing furs was too hot and her boy had sweated and itched, Yukka gathered wool from the barbed wire fences that marked the start of the foot alps and wove her boy a fine light shirt and trousers, though she hadn't ever needed such things herself, her heart, she said, being part-made of Edgelands earth so that its best temperature was hers. The deacon still always ran cold, so she now peeled back furs only for him.

The deacon felt the fine shirt as he helped his son into it and marvelled at the lightness of the weave. He told the boy about the Hasting-Elliots, the only merino folks he knew from town and who had had a fine library up at their station that he'd seen in his active deaconing days. The boy would ask and ask again to know this tale, too, of the people who grew what his fine clothes were made of, and of how he now looked so much like them.

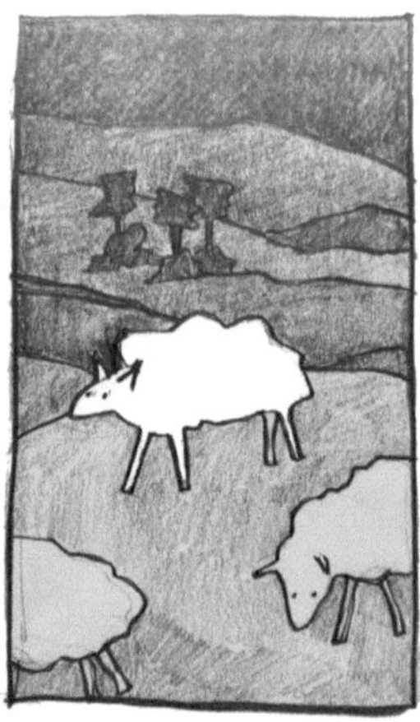

And with time passing, down in Dregs, the shock of the loss of the deacon started to fade, and old rhythms returned to the town. Boys on farms took on tailing and learning to scan paddocks for cast sheep and to shoot in low light. In Dregs proper, on the flats, boys vied for jobs running with the milk and rubbish trucks, getting strong in the rugby off-season. For the first time in as long as anyone could remember, hunters all returned safe and, though the deacon was still remembered in prayers, as was the child, the town learned to turn away from dwelling too much on the woe. Gretchen Stewart married a man from the Dip and, in time, would raise up her own family of boys. And for the first summer since the deacon had been taken, at Guy Fawkes crackers again lit the sky. Smells of gunpowder and sulphur and ash.

The boy caught the scent and asked his father, who told stories of candy floss and apples and wheels for winning chocolate and explained about sugar. And the boy said 'please we must go, dad, please get us down there'.

The deacon's legs no longer carried such rot, so he figured they might have a chance and he nodded to the boy. He figured the boy had a right. He whispered to his son, 'We'll get out of here, my boy, we'll get you there to your people'. Though as Yukka ushered them back into the cave that night, he let himself lean back into her hand.

The next day, after Yukka's hunt and thar for breakfast, she returned to the cave as usual to doze. The deacon scooped up his son and they ran.

Yukka woke to the smell of them gone and the light. Her pupils pulled back to pinpoints and though she tried to blink out the sun, for a moment she just couldn't see. As she ran her eyes streamed. The deacon, holding his son, ran hard as he could, but Yukka was strong and swifter. She smelled her way to them, caught them back up in her arms and snarled them back home, rolling the boulder behind them. In the cave she checked and checked the boulder and barely slept all that long afternoon.

She wouldn't let them out alone again.

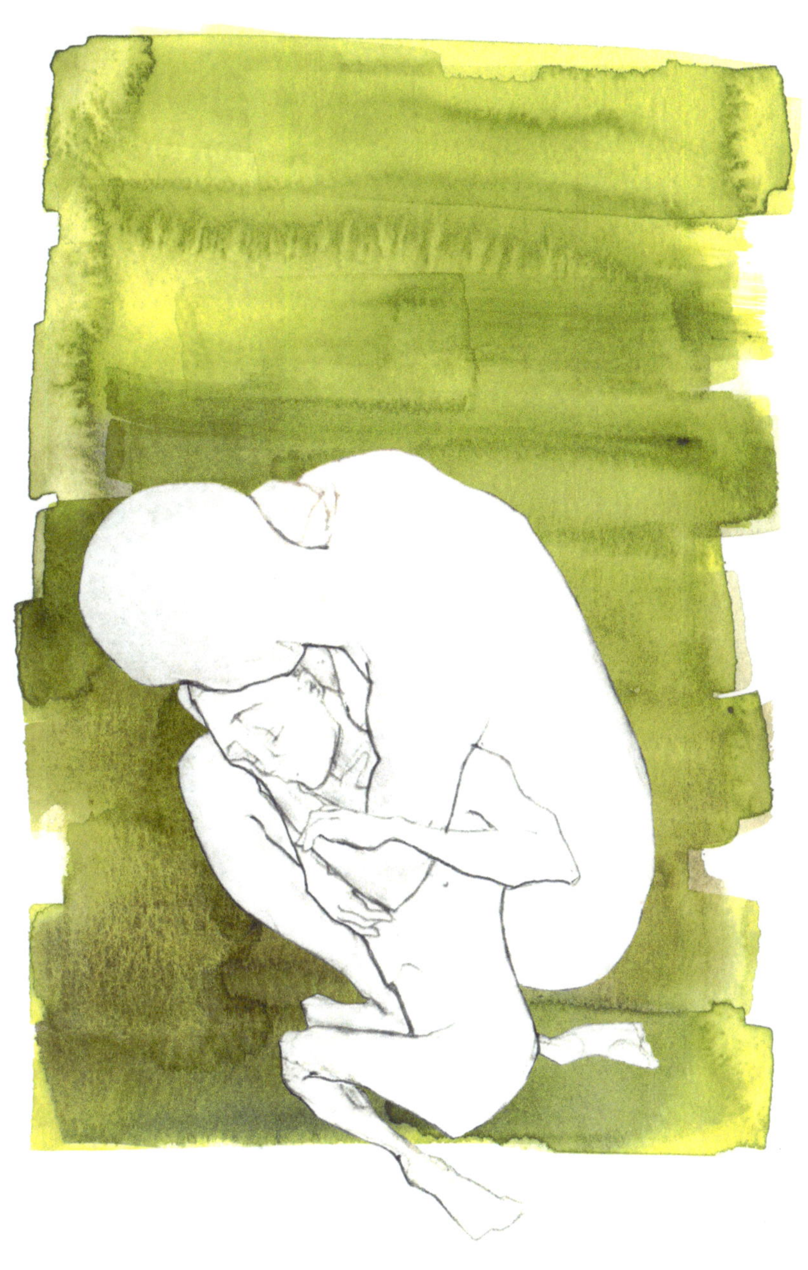

From that time on it was harder to separate mother from dad. Although Yukka would still send them out in the light under her watch, the deacon seemed to long to be back in the cave. The boy would try to urge his dad back awake, reminding him that the people, their people, were down there in the light, but the deacon would shut his eyes and curl up by his wife, even though he never could truly sleep in the day.

In the dark between his day-sleeping mother and his listless though never still dad, the boy somehow kept growing stronger, fingers pushing out into the cracks of light, his marrow taking on flavours of blue dawn, golden high noon, and the orange-purple dusk, dreaming the warmth in through his skin. Days passed and he grew so that Yukka could smell the boy's strength and became wary of the boulder. In the pre-dawn, she hunted nearby, running back quickly at small sounds, at times with just rabbits, which they ate with berries from the mouth of the cave.

And it seemed the boy learned to eat sound, and he strained at the cave cracks on the evenings that music rose up from the town. And another November came and again there were fires and he remembered what his father used to say about chocolate and apples and wheels made for winning. And with the gunpower scent he filled up with longing and his muscles lurched into decision, certain from his hamstrings to his enraged piriformis. He swore that, once he got out, it would be light only and forever. He whispered to his dad.

'We're going to go. I'll carry you.'

Surely his dad would reform in the sun.

With her son calm all that week, Yukka hunted further and returned again with goat and then chamois and then a great buck thar. Full for the first time in months, she slept. The boy crept to the boulder, pushed his shoulder against it, and it budged. He slung his father over his shoulder and ran, with a shiver of disgust at the dampness of his dad. The deacon closed his eyes to the bright of the sun but the boy held tight and ran straight and hard.

Yukka woke to light filling the cave and smelled that they'd gone before she could see it. She ran out into the wall of sun, blinded, again needing her nose to catch up with their trail. But her boy was fast, even weighed as he was by his dad. Down through the shingle her son roared, sure-footed and solid and fleet. His father's sweat, chilled and anxious, mixed with his own, clean and hot, and he shivered, but still he held tight to his dad and kept on straight down the hillside through the tussocks and flax and gorse.

Yukka howled as they tore away faster and, as the boy leapt the lime creek, she stopped still. Her loves now gone from the Edgelands.

At that creek where she couldn't go any further, it being the edge of the lands that loved her, she stood and watched as they sped down to Dregs. When they crossed through the eucalypts that marked the start of the farmland on the edge of Dregs proper, a great crack opened her sternum and she found that her thin steely aorta, a gift from the Edgelands itself, came free from the cavity with ease. It gleamed in the sun. She ached that there was nothing that could be done for her husband, but the shimmering band could be for the boy. She held it out to throw across the creek, in case he would turn back for it. But weak as she was by then, it fell into the creek, where it washed away, over stones and past eddies, flowing out to the sea.

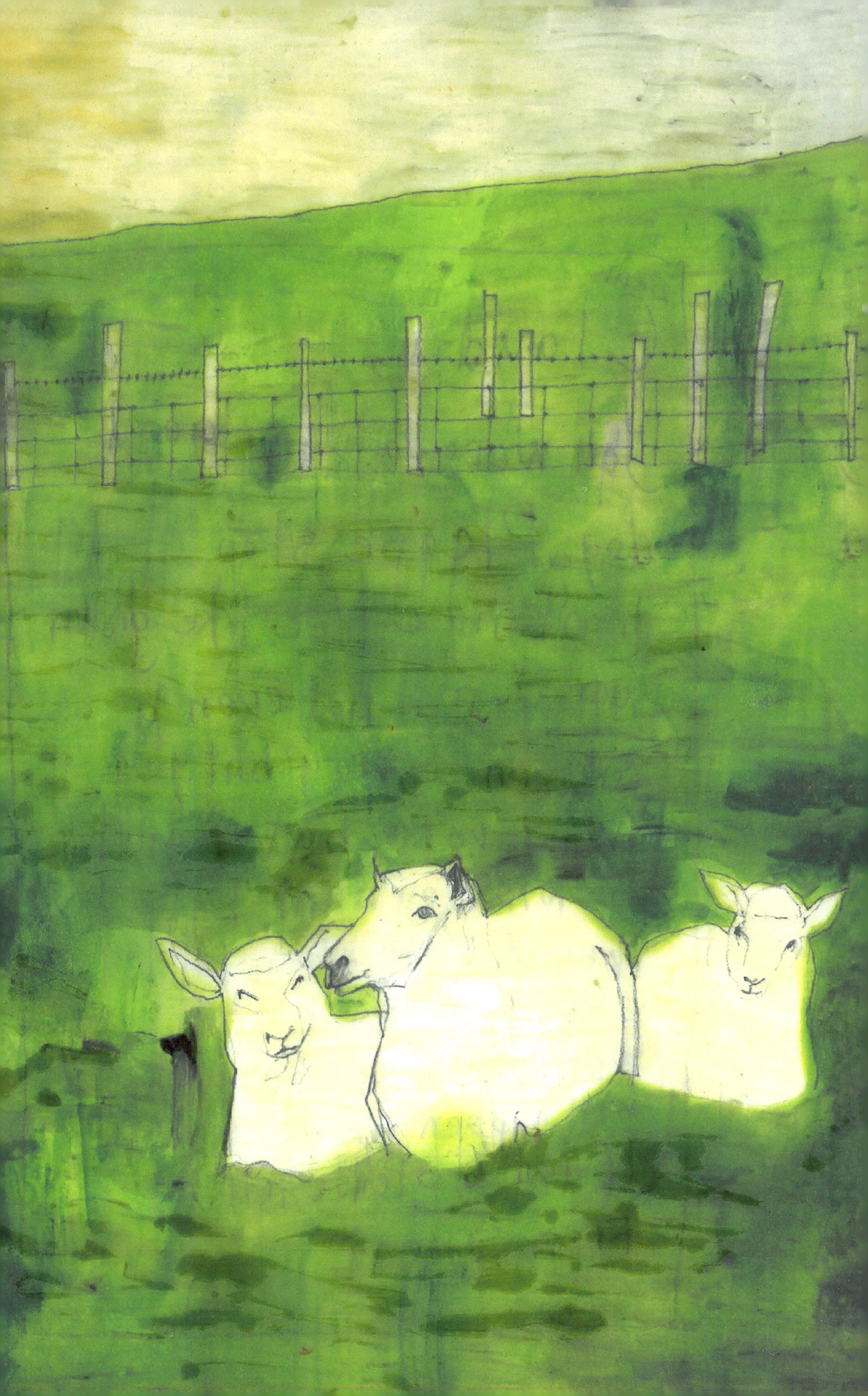

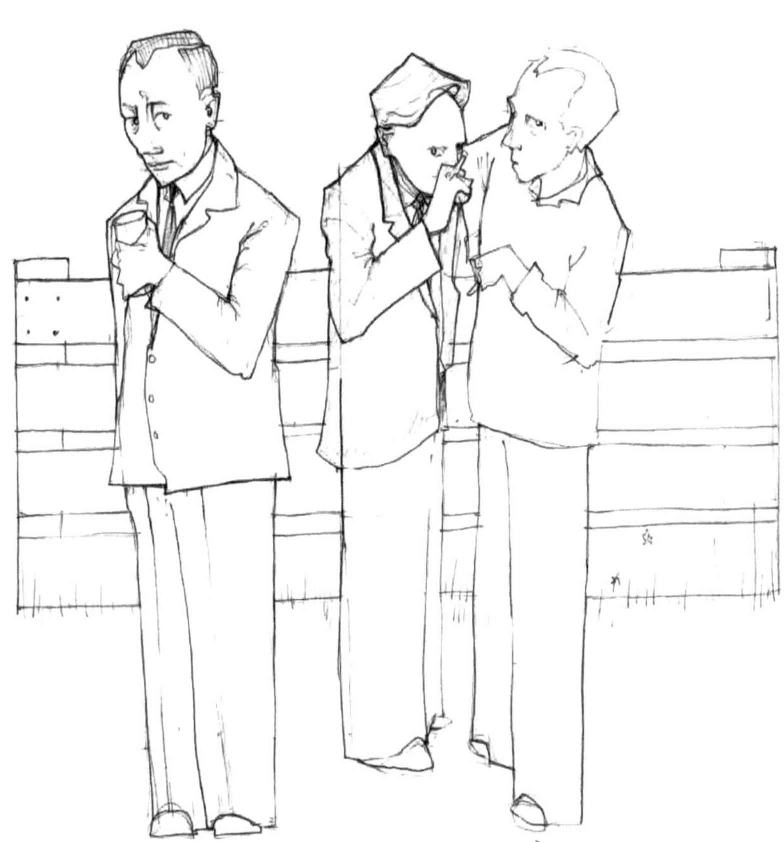

Six simple tips on processing viral rabbits

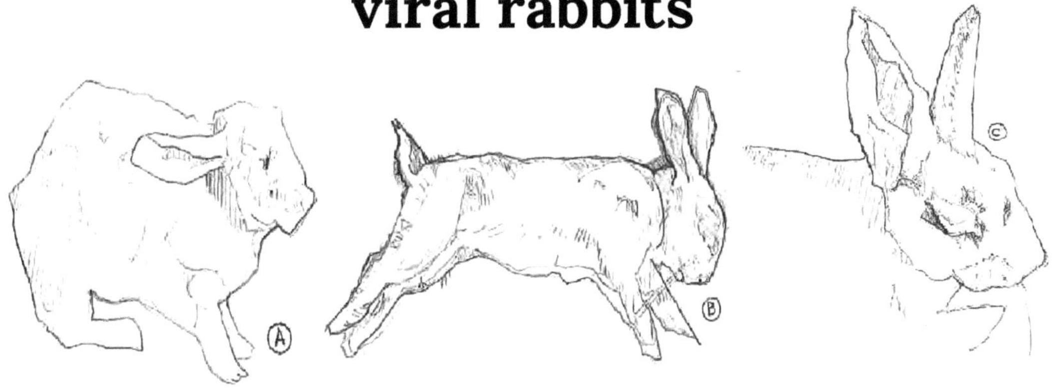

1. There is no health requirement to remove the damaged part of your rabbit carcass before consumption. Although both myxomatosis and rabbit calicivirus disease (RCD) are potent neurotoxins in rabbits, for humans they are completely harmless.

2. If you are still concerned, heating the carcass to 70 degrees Celsius will reliably destroy any viral residue.

3. The characteristic myxomatotic eye decay (see images A, B and C) is particularly easy to remove.

4. All natural eyes must be replaced in taxidermy, regardless of condition, making mounting an even easier way to process mildly myxomatosed carcasses.

5. Please see Dregs and Surrounds Council Code of Health, Section 3.4.12, for further guidelines regarding taxidermy.

6. Severely decayed carcasses can be spread as bait to further reduce rabbit numbers and help return profitability to your local area.

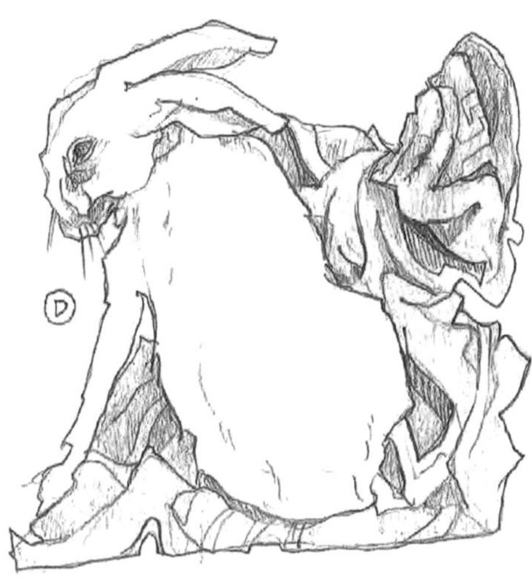

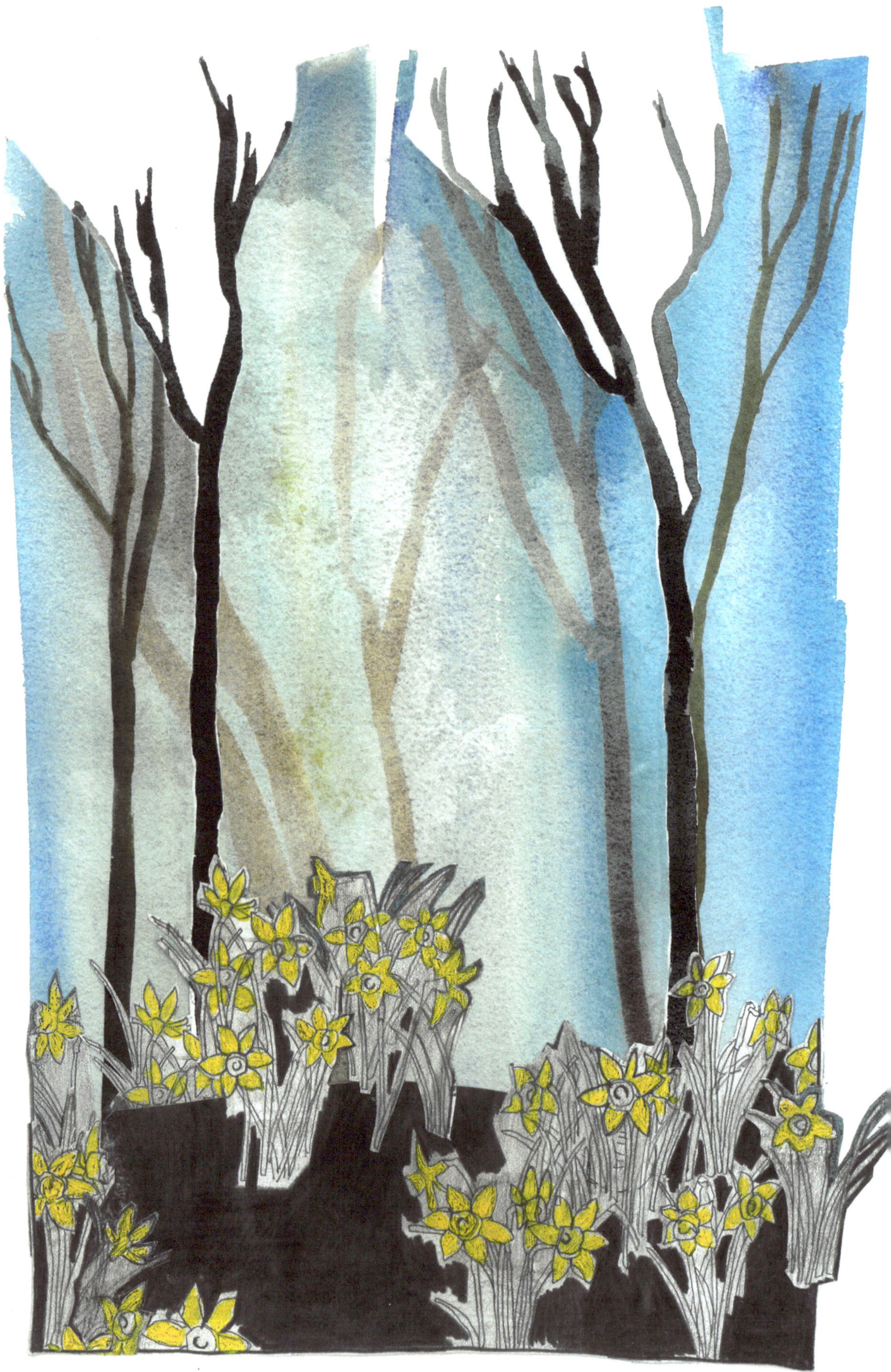

Very pale boy

In one of those times when strangers were shifting to Dregs by choice, a very pale boy arrived. Him and his very fair brothers, one older, one younger, his light willowy mum, whose rare emergence from their house caused quite a stir, and his ruddy sharemilker dad. The boys were the types you'd expect to get teased until they peed on the mat in Room 8, and then you'd make them pay for the rest of their lives, even if they left Dregs and got rich and then for some reason came back with all that money. That sort of kid is usually easy to spot, being very slight or slightly fatty or very fair, curly or red. But this boy, the middle one of the three pale boys, and who didn't speak, not for the whole time he was in Dregs, was never teased by anyone. Neither were his brothers, except the youngest, and that was only lightly, fondly.

Gaylene Metcalfe was strong and swift and golden. At 11 she could already manage her father's herd and was proudly in charge of the great silage mound that sat, tarpaulined, out the front of the Metcalfe property. The fermented hay was full of goodness and took care of the Metcalfe's herd over the full of even the fiercest winters.

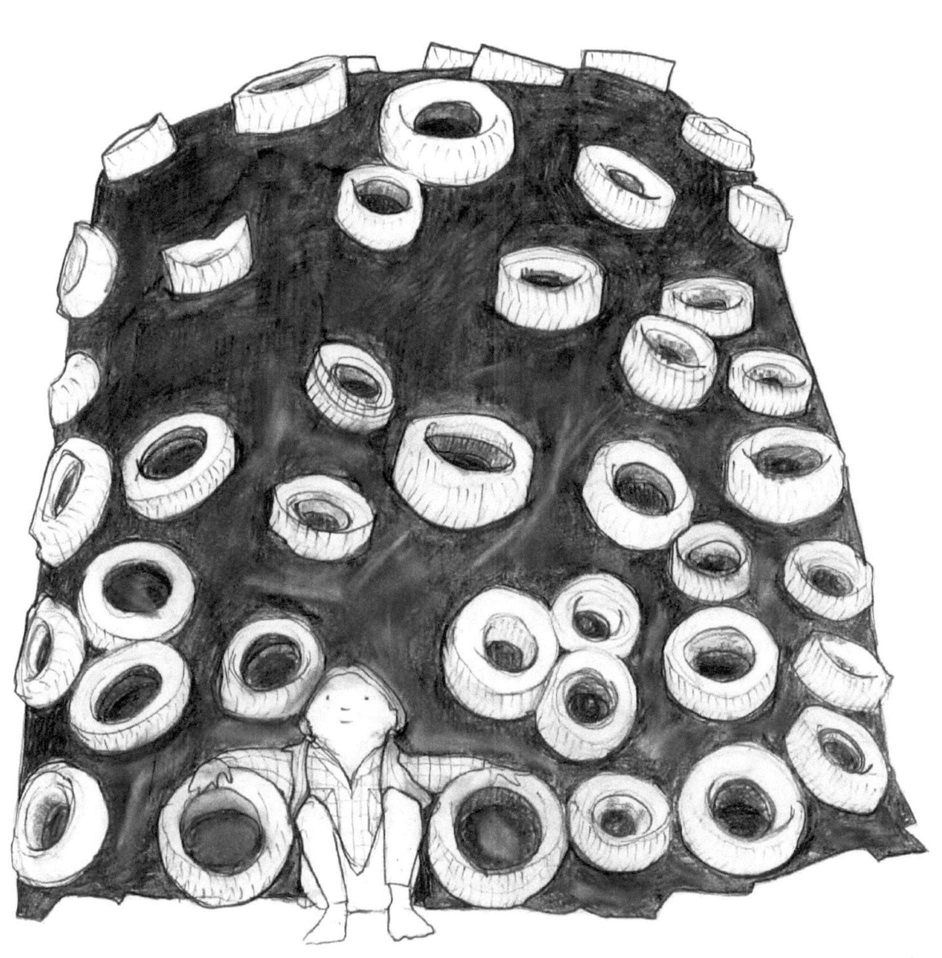

Today, with the rumour of a newcomer, the rest of the kids in Room 8 had been careful not to leave gaps at their tables, filling empty seats with bags and books and lunches, but Gaylene figured the new kid would have to sit somewhere and left the empty seat beside her empty. And the very pale boy was put next to her.

And the very pale boy didn't speak, so, in that morning lesson, they failed the pair assignment on Tuatara relocation. Gaylene kept talking towards this quiet fellow at her table, oblivious to the looks of her classmates and to Mr Allen's shushes. She talked at the boy until he wrote her small notes of things so filthy she'd never thought to think of them, even though she'd grown up with cows and shit and milking and was well known in Dregs for being a feral girl, even if she was good with keeping the books. There was something so delicate in the very pale boy that Gaylene almost didn't believe the notes could say what they did. And without the resistance she might have built up in herself, had he not been so pretty and slight, the little notes navigated their way up to a secret pocket she'd made for just such messages. And, back at home, Gaylene forgot little things, like, in the morning milking, which tit first into the cluster.

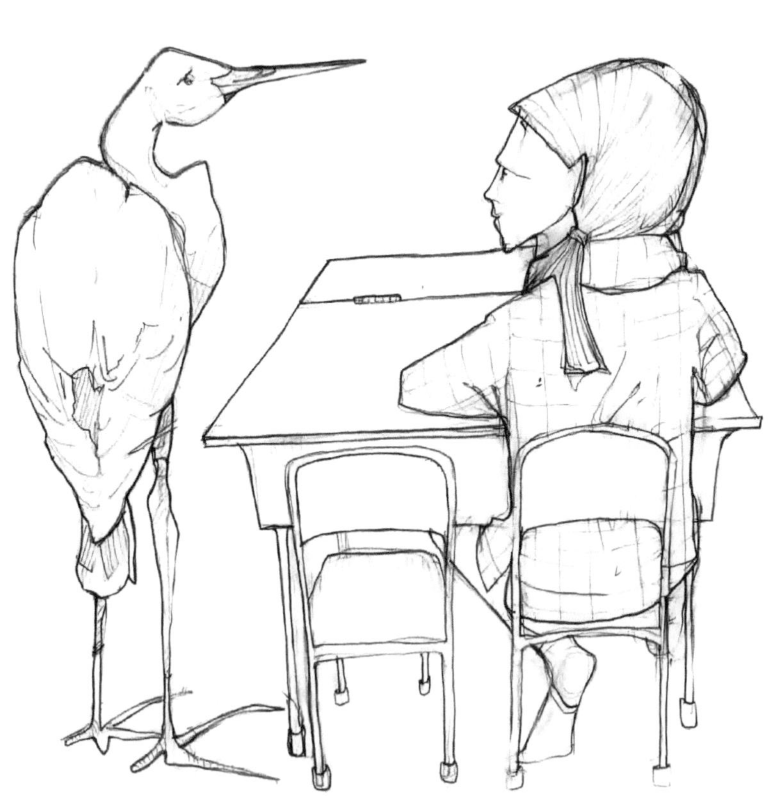

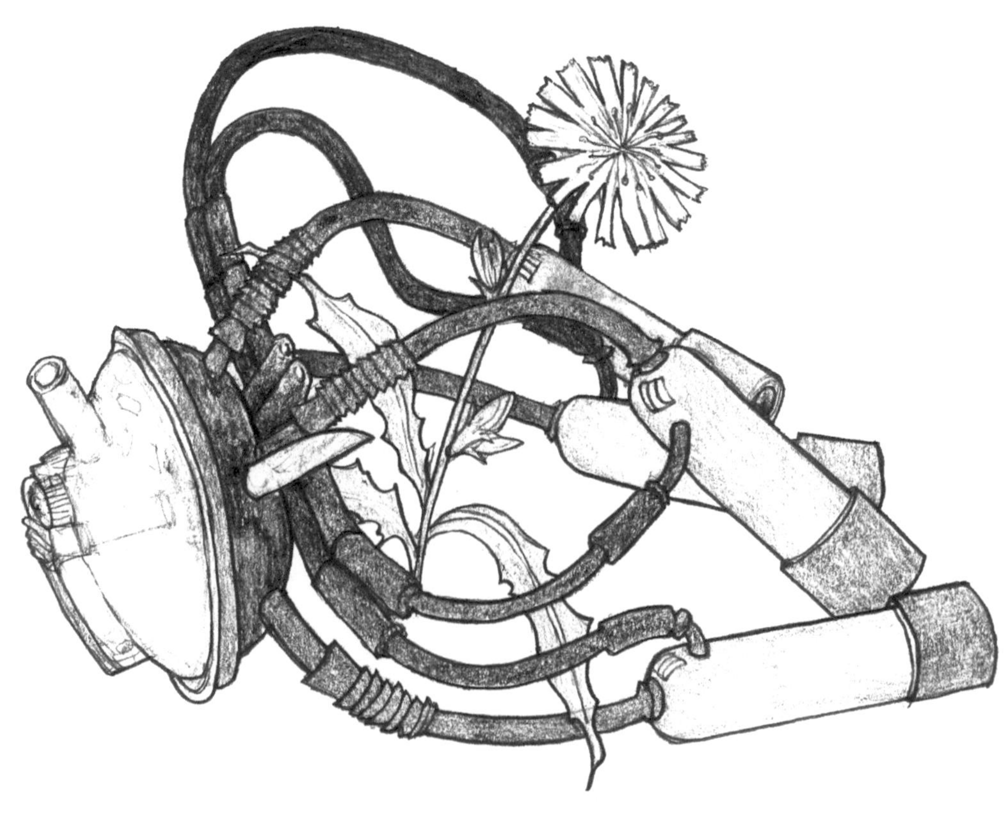

No-one else received the notes that Gaylene did. But other children, without knowing why, would sidle up to the very pale boy and quietly sniff at his forearms. Once, two bolder students, Stewie Lyttle and Fisher, got so close they could smell him just there between his fingers where a small scent extruded that was very difficult to pass by without being caught up for just a moment. But when the boy stood, always at the edge of a group, even when he'd been around for a while and people would've been happy to have him anywhere, his arms were stiff and awkward and his fingers were splayed and Gaylene wanted like anything to shove them back in his pockets so they wouldn't be so all out in the open.

But when he was seated opposite, with the smell of the lily girl drifting between them, Gaylene relaxed along with his hands, which sat one alight the other, the left protecting the right. Gaylene reached under her half of the table for the pile of wet pink gum, now banned from Dregs Normal, and pressed her first two fingers into it until the mound became warm and soft and she hid her fingers in the moist cocoon, and kept them there as she watched the very pale boy's very still hands.

The surrounding gum piles, excluded from this nest, crawled up further into the table boards and wedded their polymers into the wood.

But all this was a long time ago now.

Being a girl good with books and yet with forearms resolute to hold any frantic bobby calf you could name, it was only natural that Gaylene would be courted by someone with work enough to make the most of her. David Michaels, of fat fingers and straight calves, knew he'd have acres to run when his father got old. He knew that although Gaylene was only 11 you had to get in early. He'd learnt from old Fat Jones who'd had his eye on Matilda Eddie all those years, even though she was flat-chested and had no aptitude for long-range planning. And even though you'd have thought there wouldn't be a competition, one morning, before old Fat got started on his courtship in earnest, it seems Hayden Green had woken thinking of Matilda and had filled her innards with seed and they sprouted, so that was that, and Fat lost her, and Hayden not being from farm people, Matilda had not just been lost from his farm, but from anyone's. So David Michaels knew that when they start to smell of iron, those new little women, you needed to work fast, even with the plain ones. He went to visit Gaylene's people.

Mrs Metcalfe's top was purple with the blackberries she'd gathered after jogging down by Chisholm River. Dribbles ran down to her shorts as David Michaels waved her down. He'd just come from discussing Gaylene with George Metcalfe, Mrs Metcalfe's eldest. George was tighthead prop to David's loose, which gave the pair ample time to talk as they waited for scrums to be packed. Rich Mulvey, their hooker, was dim and not inclined to gossip, so they'd sorted out the whole of the courtship as they propped through that afternoon training. David Michaels explained the arrangements to Mrs Metcalfe as the stain dripped past her knee. They walked back to the farm and found Mr Metcalfe, who placed his arm on his damp wife's shoulder. They toasted the man come courting their girl.

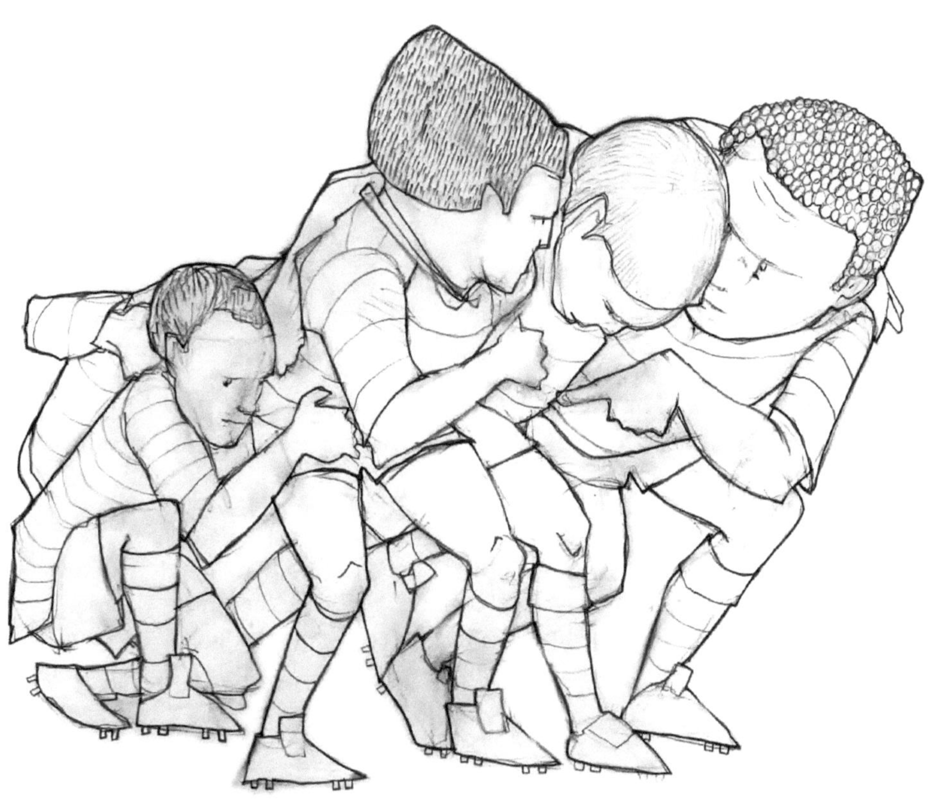

But even so, and although the ruddy sharemilking of the very pale boy's father hadn't been going so well and it looked as though they'd need to leave Dregs in not too long, the very pale boy would walk in from Cliffstock nightly to see Gaylene. The time this takes is known from the time Alice and red Rachel M. walked from the edge of North Dregs to the Southdown Rise Annual Rodeo.

Though it had been worth it for the Sex Pistols CD they'd found on the verge of State Highway One, which they'd listened to and listened to at Alice's because she'd had a CD player, and which had changed them both so that it came to seem almost inevitable they'd move out of the district, it had been a long, long walk and they'd nearly missed the rodeo. It had taken a full three hours to walk it in the daytime with water and when they could see their footing just fine. The very pale boy would walk the distance dry in the night and arrive at Gaylene's on the other side of Dregs, out in the Southdown Rise, where her people have always been. They would rub up on each other, him and Gaylene, and little spots of heat from their rubbing singed brown into their sides so they'd move and start again until the spots became too many for them to have somewhere comfortable to sit. They rested in the soft patch of lamb's ear out the back of the holding bay until it was time for them both to leave for milking.

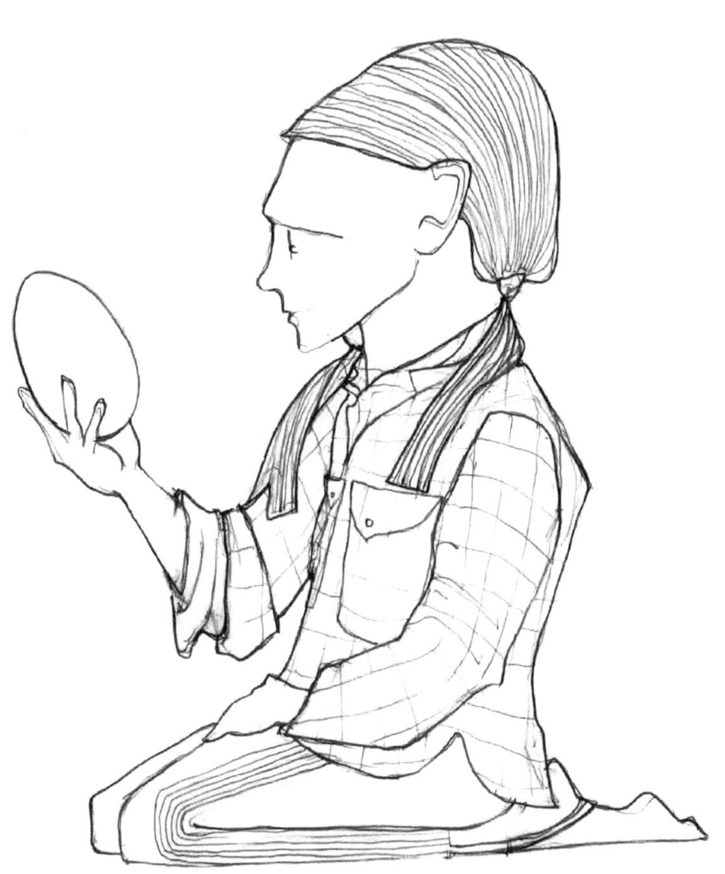

Mr and Mrs Metcalfe caught the smell of the very pale boy, but he was a sharemilker's son. And sharemilkers and their families were as likely to pass on through Dregs as not, so they waited for them to pass by. And when the very pale boy did leave, along with his brothers and mother and sharemilker dad, people didn't throw rumours after them, as they did with the rest. They just sat outside the Royal Hotel at the tables on the Green and watched them fly off. David Michaels stayed back at his farm. As the family flew over the Western Dip, he shot up into the air one round at a time and then went to help Gaylene with the milking.

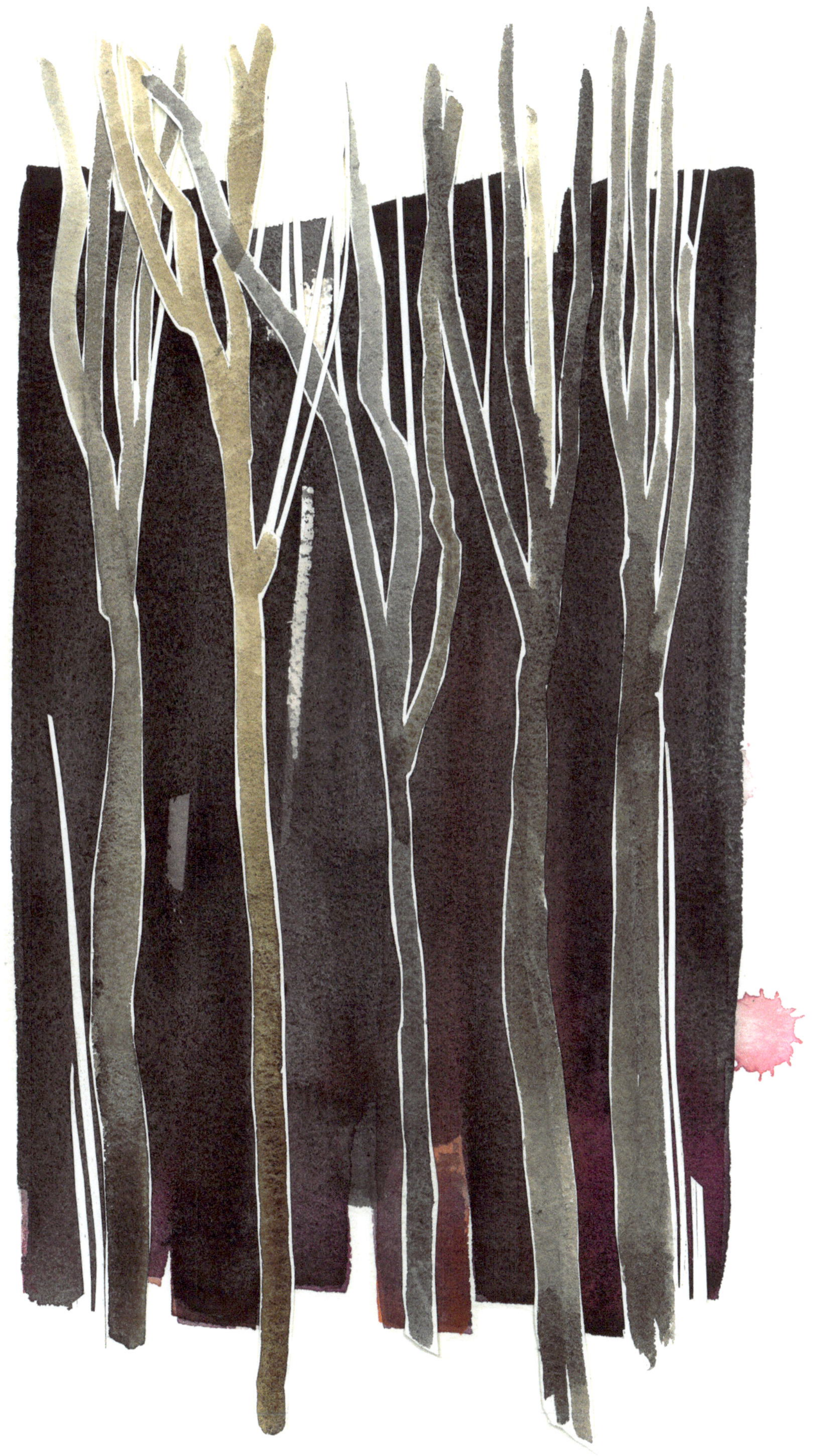

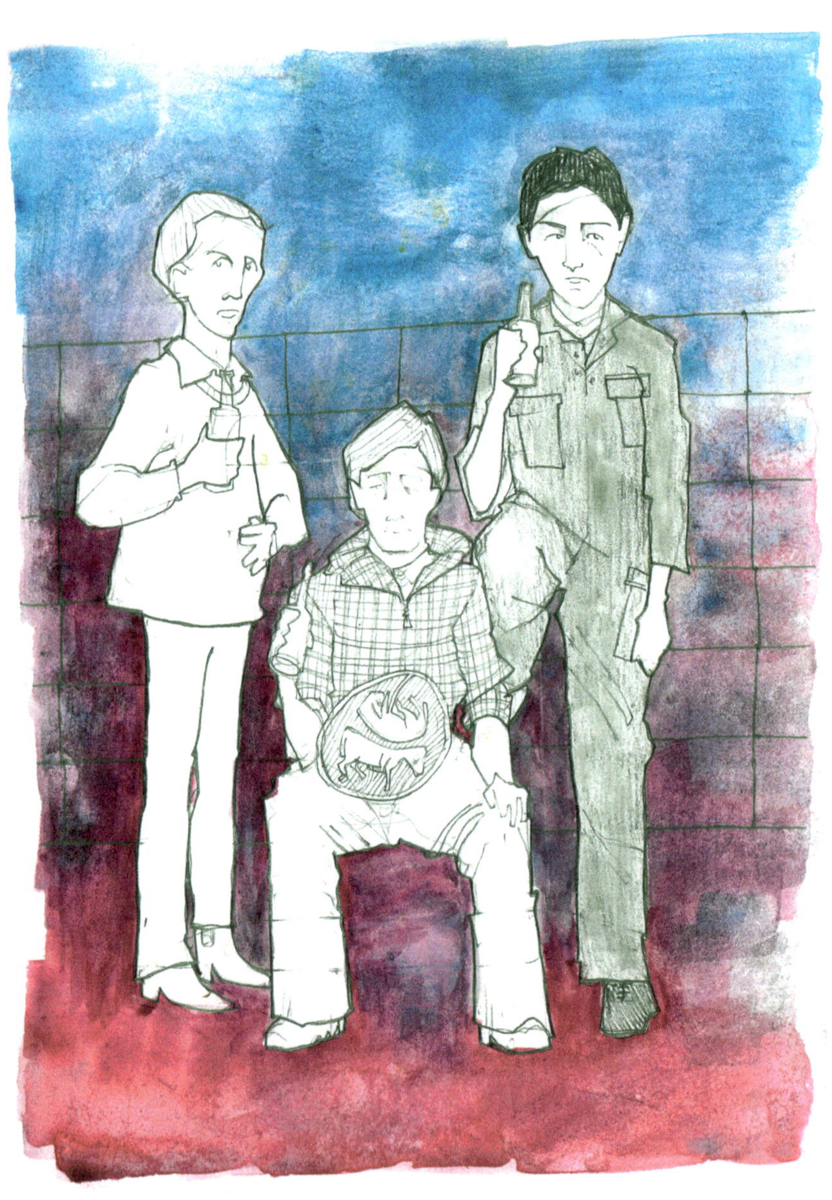

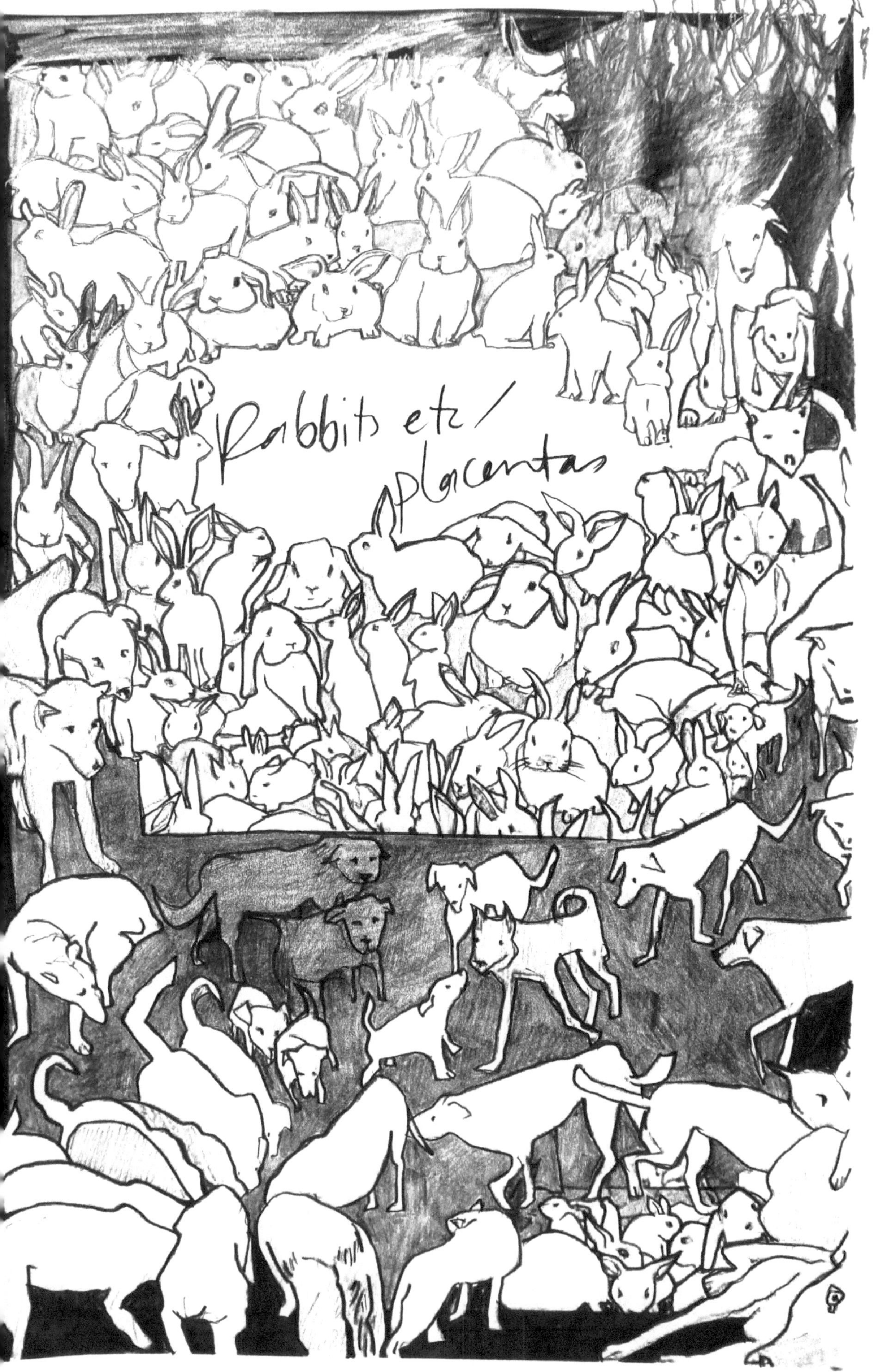

Rabbits etc/
placentas

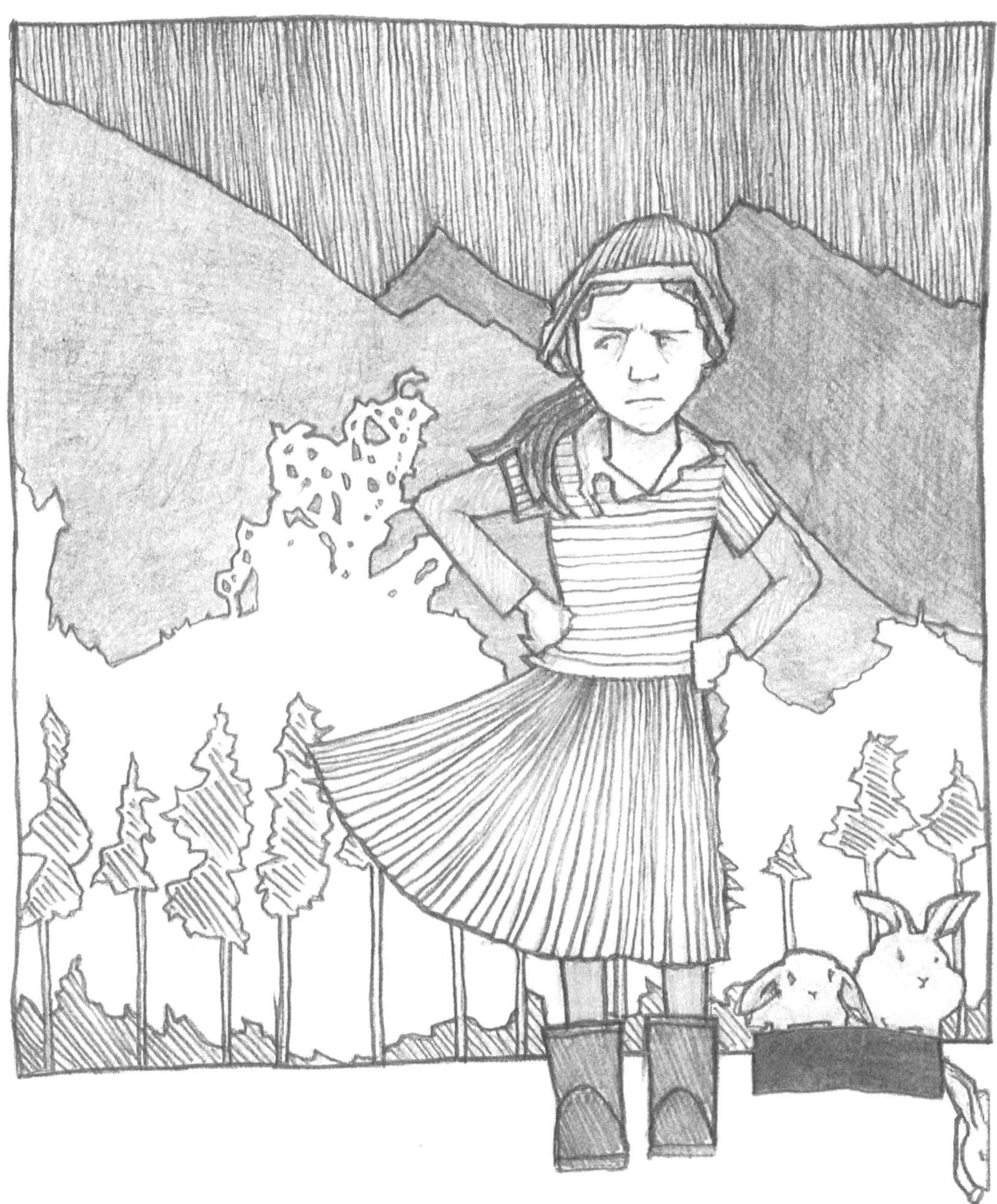

When rabbits took over the McKercher farm, Mr McKercher brought Hannah and Nick back home from school for good. You never saw a brother and a sister hate each other more. What was left of the farm would be Nick's and he walked as if it were already. Hannah spat in the scone mix, and though Nick never saw her do it, he suspected. Their dad rose before dawn and took his son with him to fix the fencing, test rabbit-proof grasses, and to shoot at what rabbits they could. Mrs McKercher, who had long felt her strength waning, wondered how life might have gone had she eaten the children's placentas. How the redness of them had gleamed.

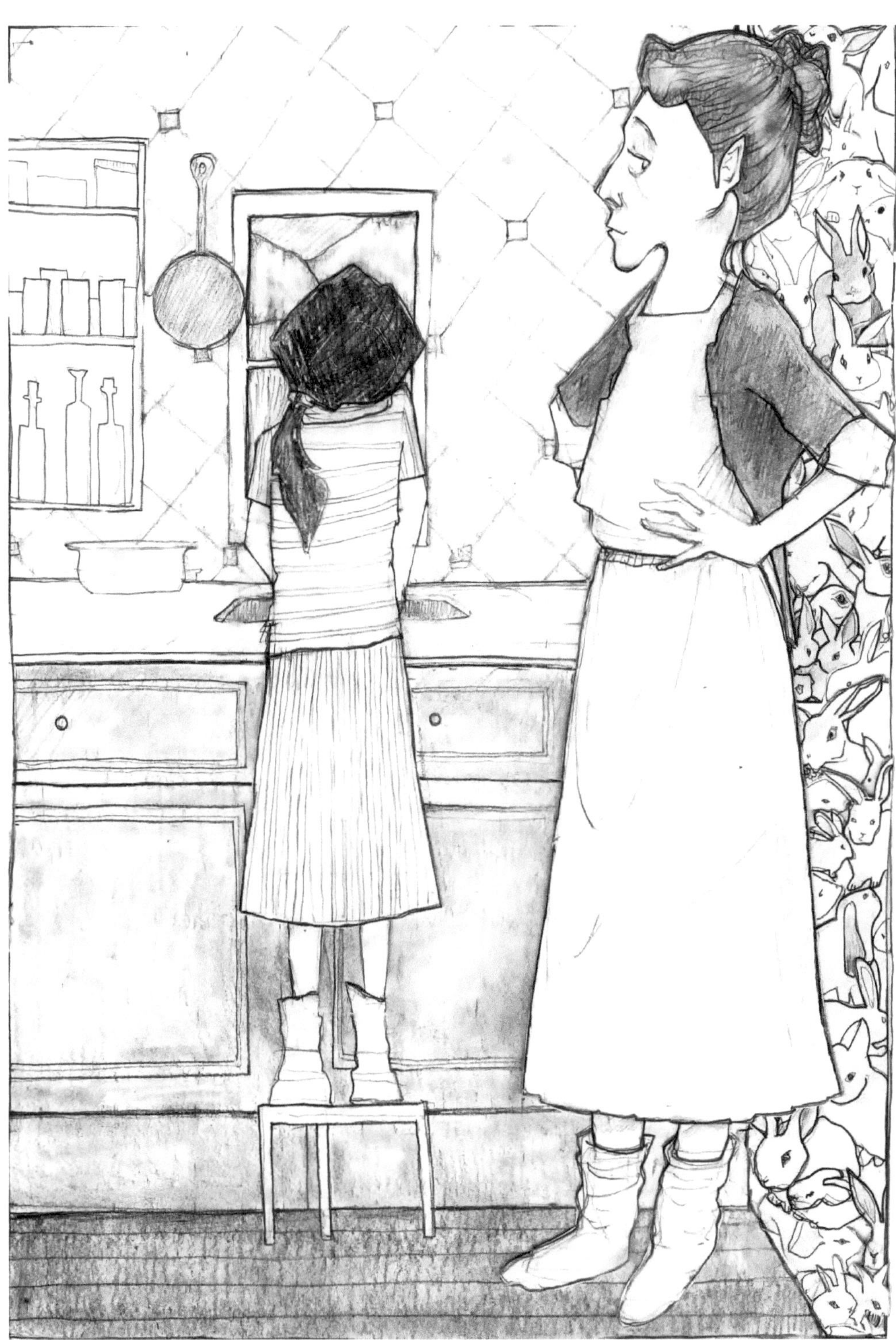

All over the farm, even with Nick and Mr McKercher out testing and trialling and trapping and shooting, and with rabbit carcasses filling the offal pit, there were rabbits and rabbits. Sheep turned to bone on the hillside.

Hannah chucked cala lily bulbs into the pit and they bloomed in three days and smelled of sweet dead rabbit. In time, the pit lured stray dogs. Eggs went missing from the hen house and the innards of spring lambs soaked into the earth (the grass grew up fine and strong the following year).

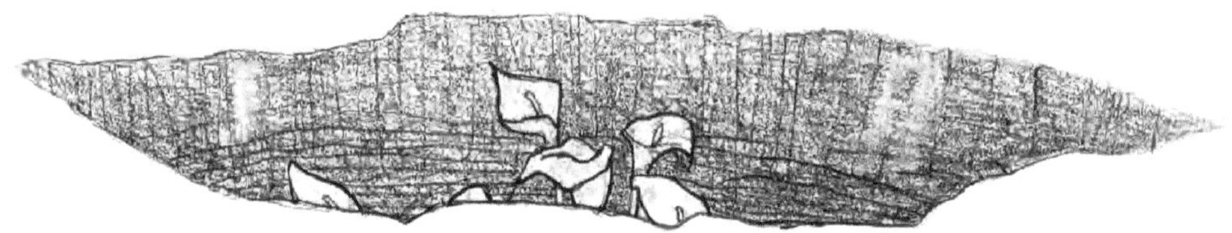

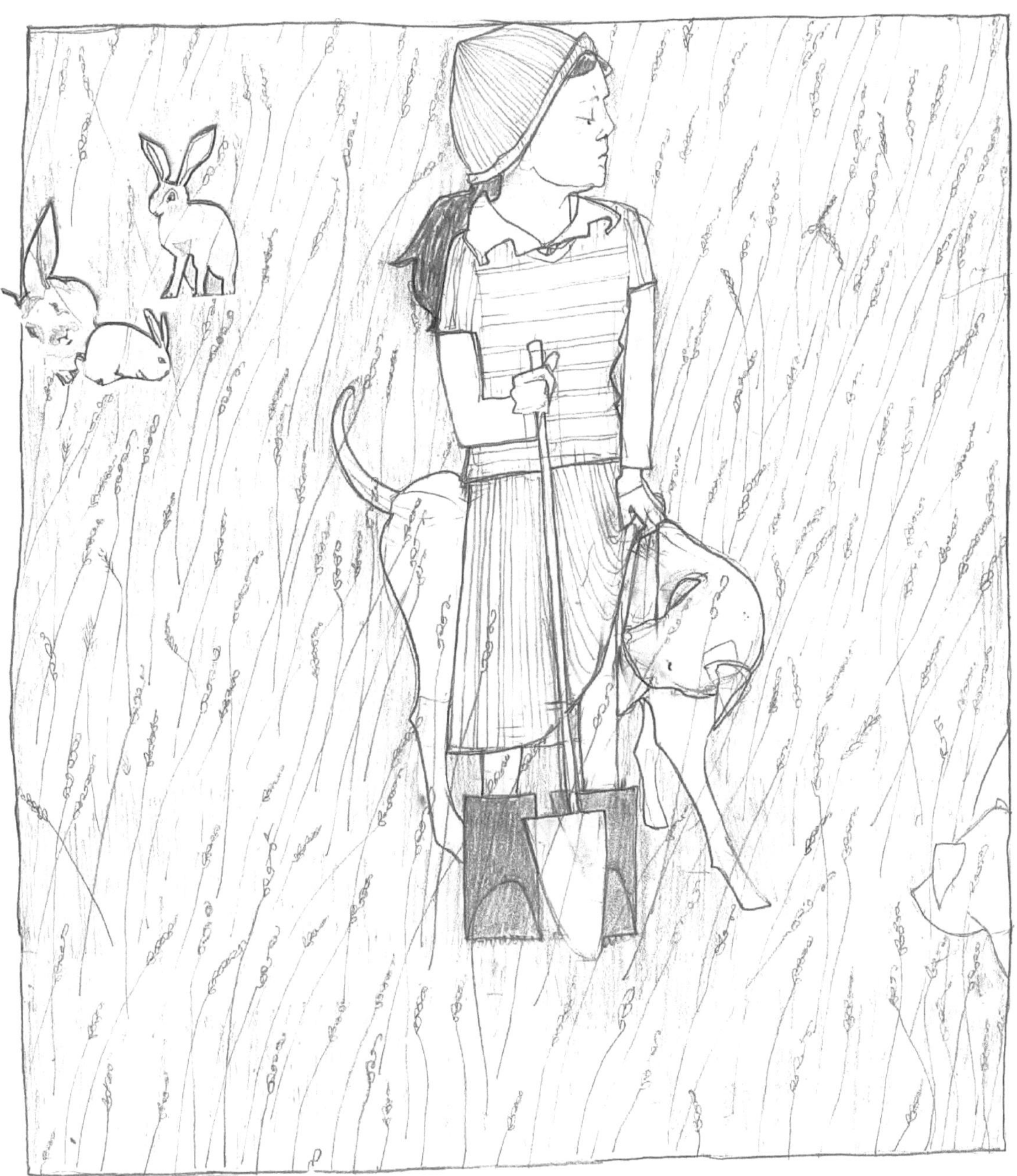

Hannah smelt the pack before she saw them, in the Timothy grass behind
the shed. They would have eaten her like they did those kids in town, but
Hannah offered up her scent and the front dog accepted. Warmth and
fur and wetness. A white-muzzled bitch snapped, but Hannah growled
her down.

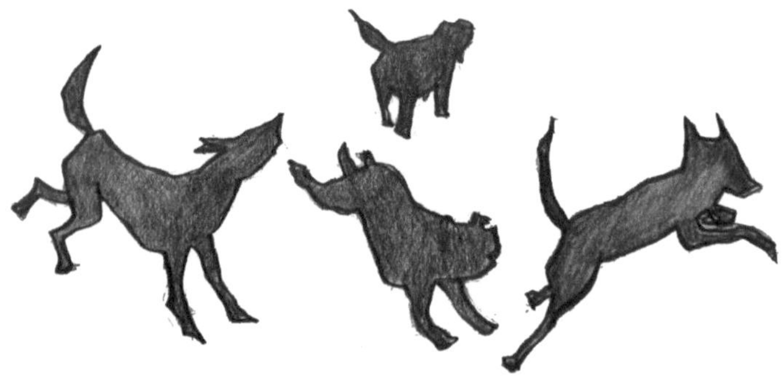

Each dawn and dusk the pack waited in the shadows of the walnut tree. They howled Hannah awake and she unlocked the back paddock gates to lead them through the crossing ditch to the yellow broom-filled scrublands at the back of the farm, slaughtering rabbits all the while. They came home satisfied and bloody-muzzled, the dogs hanging back behind the shed in the young blue fescue trial grass and Hannah curling up in her bedroom.

Inside, there was soon no room in the freezer for the bulk of the carcasses, so Hannah took just the heavy ones back to her mum. If their bodies were still warm and loose, her mother would wriggle any kits out and nip off their placentas to chew on them thoughtfully, blissfully, in the living room corner. With the strength of daily placentas, she didn't need Hannah's help inside like she used to, so she let her sleep right through the day, humming snatches of Bizet as she did the books and sorted out whatever was for tea.

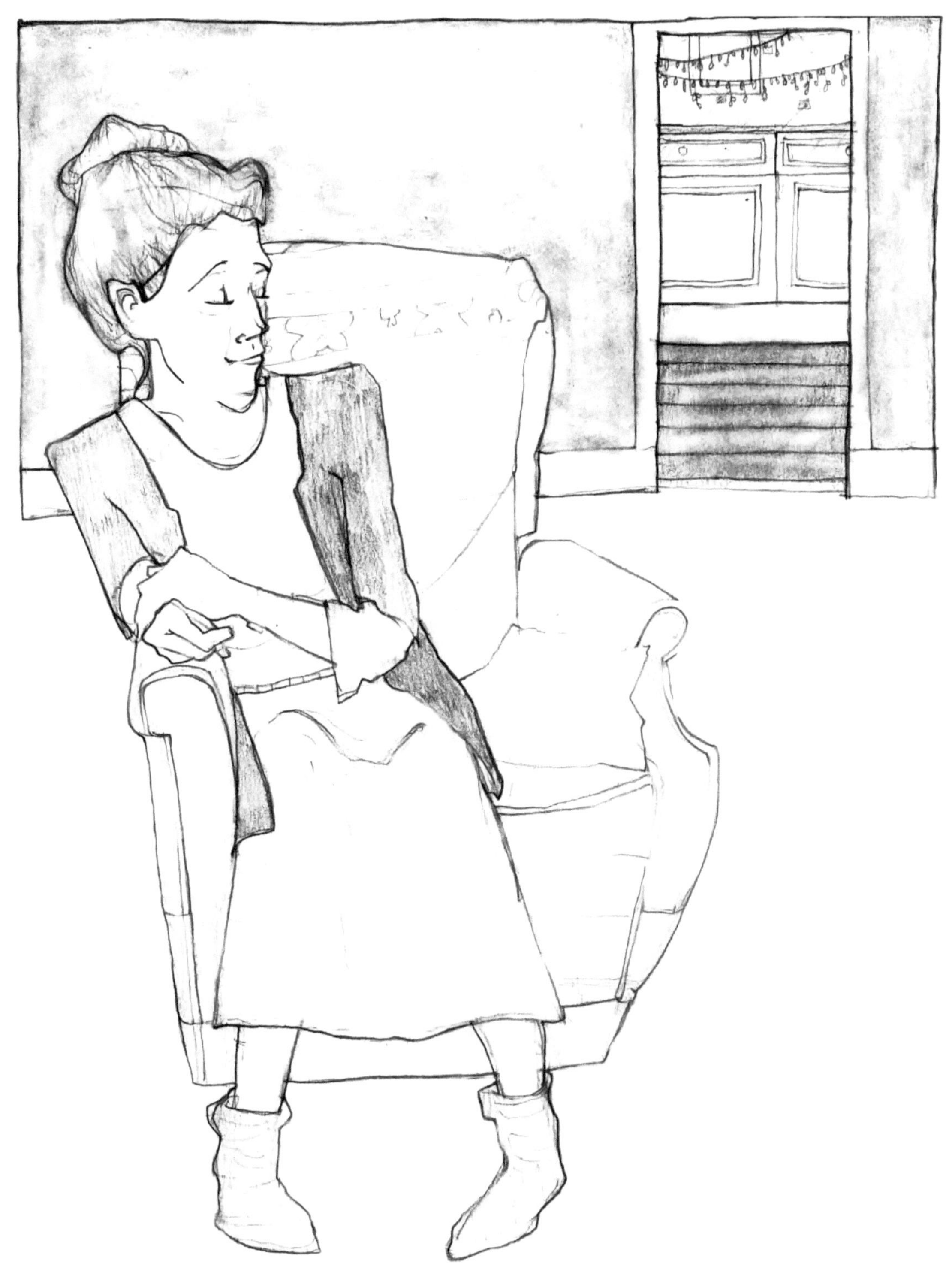

No-one asked how Hannah was bringing down the numbers, though the howling and the teeth marks in the carcasses gave clues enough. Hannah's dad and Nick figured she'd found an old half-feral sheepdog, or a grizzled trash staffy up from Dregs proper. But out alone on a drizzly Tuesday, to check on how the fescue was holding up, Hannah's dad saw the pack surrounding his daughter, not threatening but seemingly enraptured. He'd called out 'Oi! Get away!' but they raised their haunches and bared their teeth.

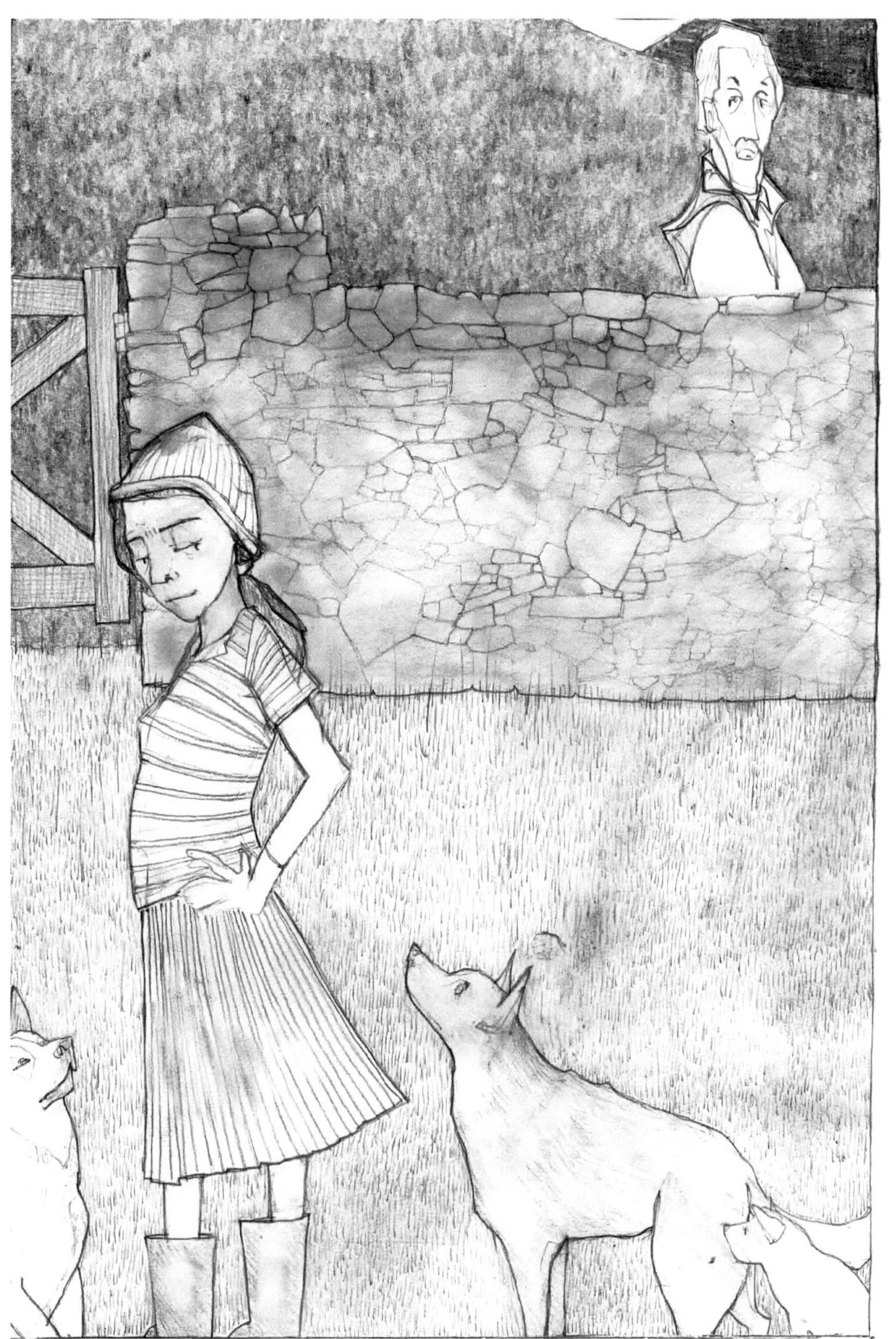

Hannah's dad called for Nick and raised his rifle, hitting the smallest in the pack, a rip-eared beagle-something cross. Nick rode into the baying dogs and lunged for his sister, but the front dog leapt and sunk his teeth into Nick's wrist and he bled. Another shot from Mr McKercher and the dogs scattered enough that he could drag Hannah into the house. He had Nick drop the beagle down the pit.

Mr McKercher locked Hannah in the pantry and took Nick to town to have his wrist checked. He'd buy an incinerator and, tomorrow, he'd fill in the offal pit, unsavoury practice as it was. Even as he wound up the car windows against the dust of the shingle road, he heard the pack howling for Hannah. He shivered as he heard her bay back.

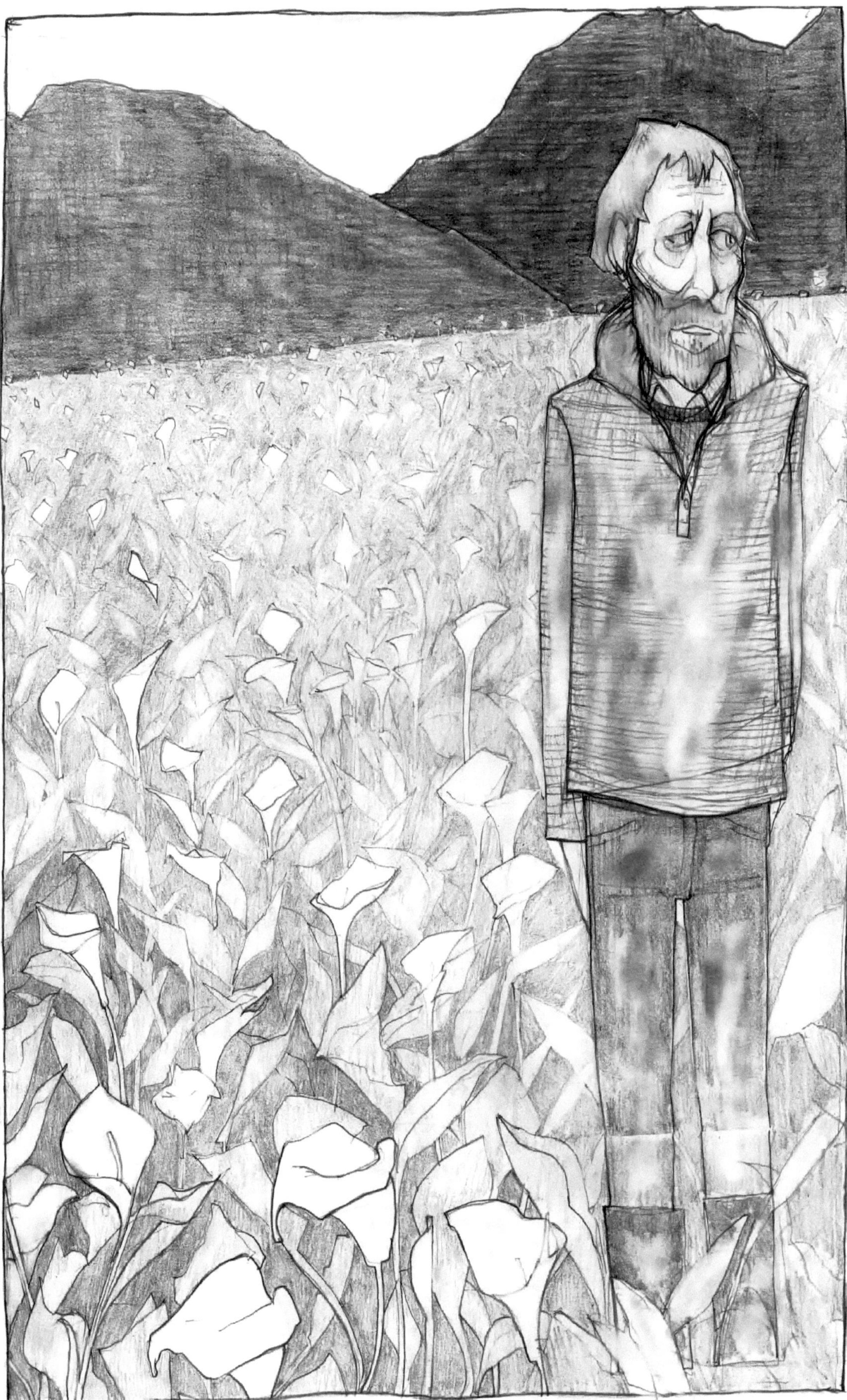

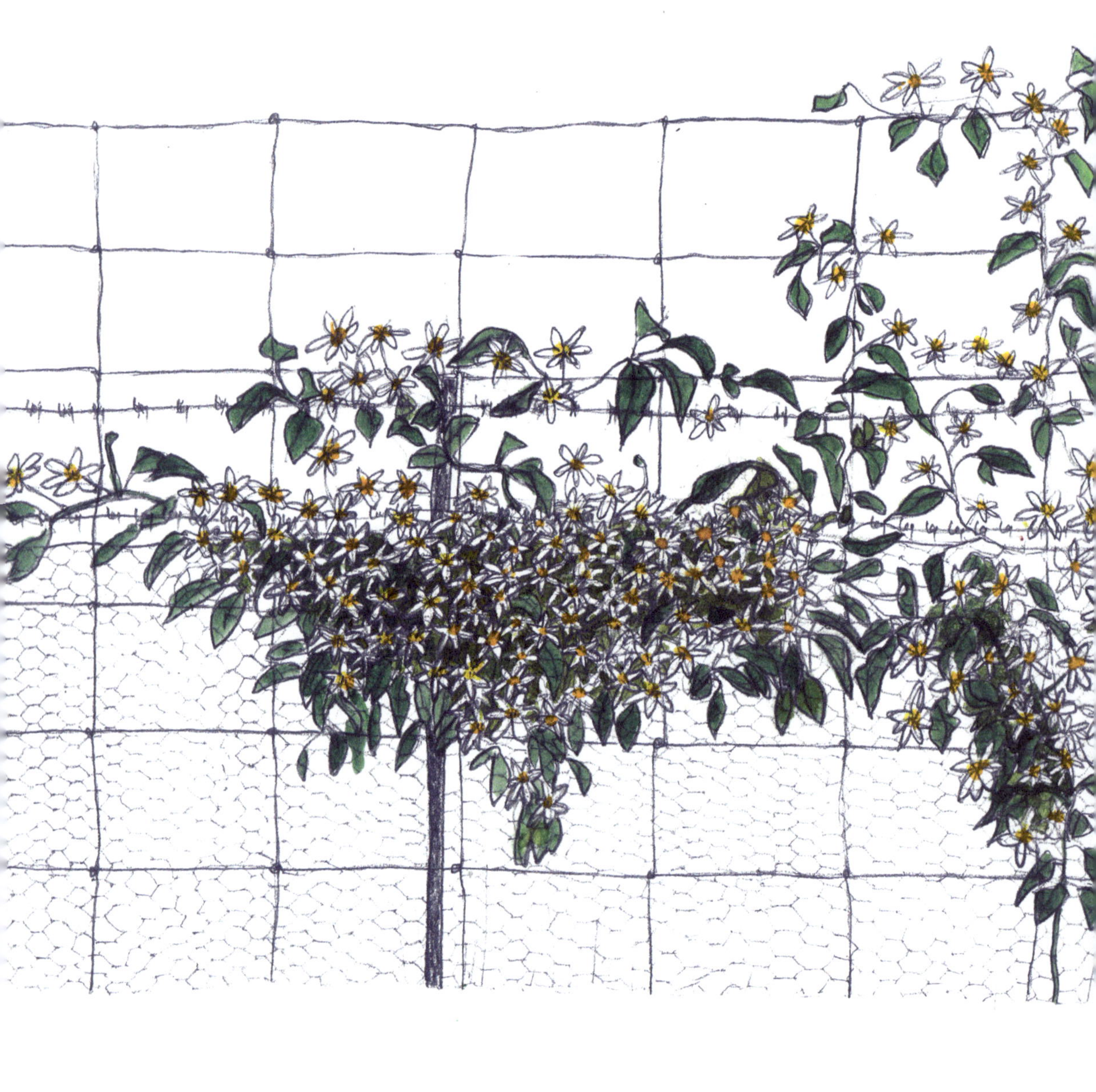

Husbandry of unusual animals and financial possibilities

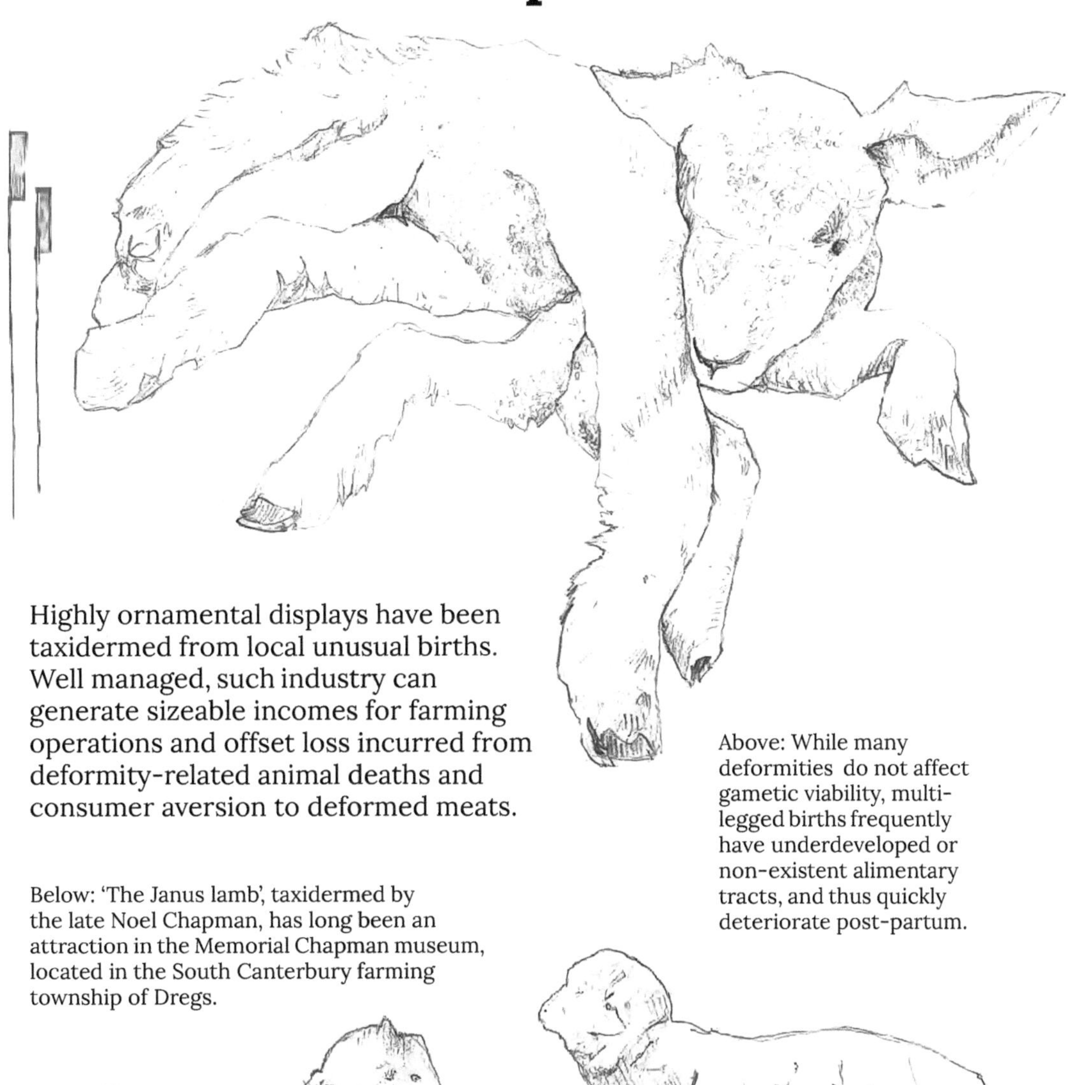

Highly ornamental displays have been taxidermed from local unusual births. Well managed, such industry can generate sizeable incomes for farming operations and offset loss incurred from deformity-related animal deaths and consumer aversion to deformed meats.

Above: While many deformities do not affect gametic viability, multi-legged births frequently have underdeveloped or non-existent alimentary tracts, and thus quickly deteriorate post-partum.

Below: 'The Janus lamb', taxidermed by the late Noel Chapman, has long been an attraction in the Memorial Chapman museum, located in the South Canterbury farming township of Dregs.

Above: Unlike animals with true supernumerous limb formations, stock with rudimentary polymelia may breed vigorously.

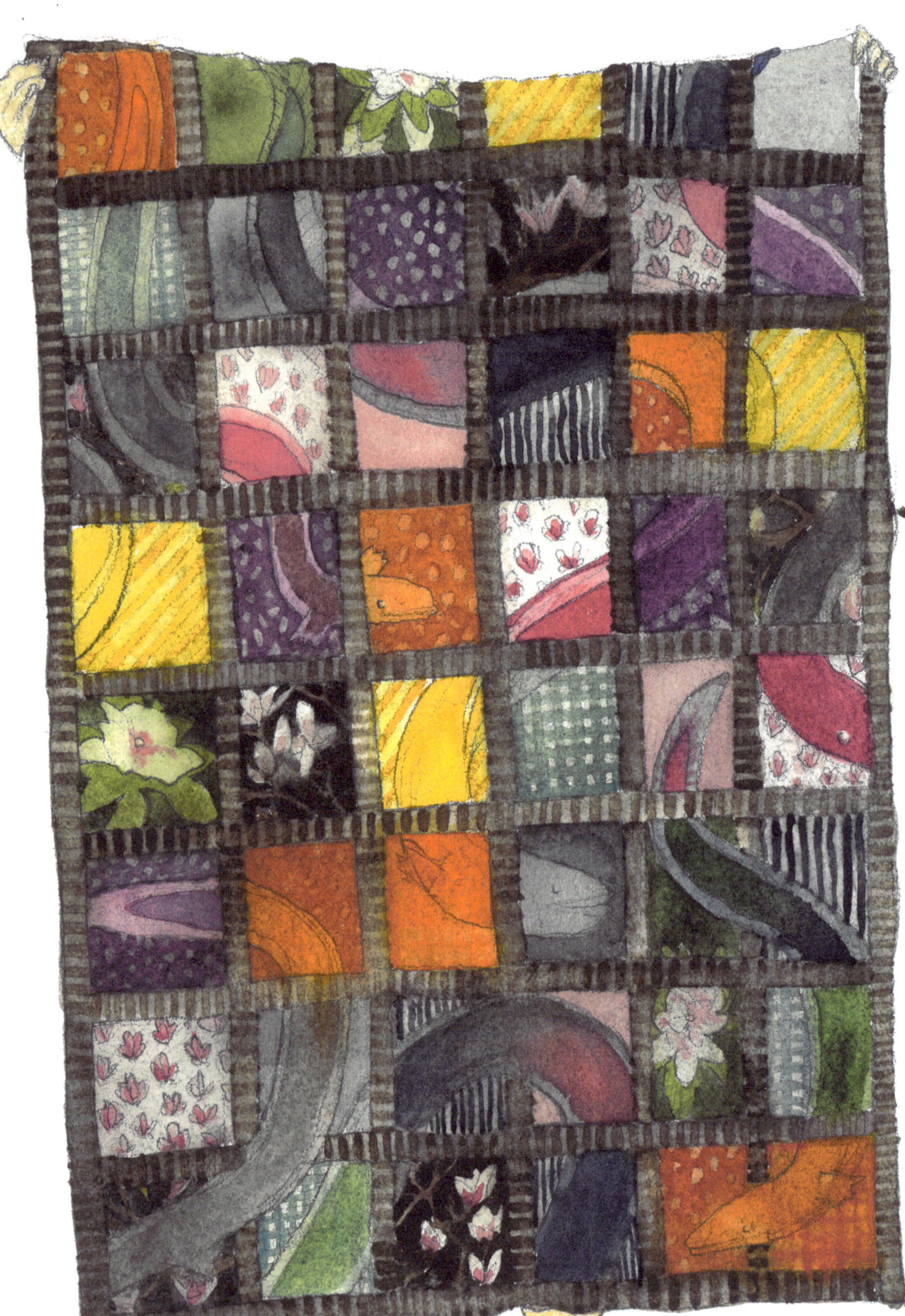

Indelible couch smell

Moira McKenzie was improving herself—with lifting things, with catching and batting, with rugby—to get fit for marrying onto a farm. She knew hired hands weren't common since the downturn, so a would-be farm wife had to prove herself ready and able to take on what jobs might come.

A fact of life she'd already accepted was that, unlike her, well-bred girls from the country don't need to prove their good fit, as they'd been moving differently right from the start. While town girls played netball in winter, and, in the summer, sunbathed or loitered about town, girls from good farms were raised to play hockey and tennis and ride. Even though few became champions of anything much, they moved in a way that was sure yet so graceful, mighty bones packed into fine wrists.

But Moira was from Dregs proper. And, as far as she knew, the only town girls like her who'd managed to marry themselves onto a farm had been champions of some kind or another. She counted the three she knew on her fingers: a skier who'd won silver at nationals, a professional whitewater rafter and a regionally-placed painter of flowers. All were now living married on farms. It wasn't a guarantee, though, this business of feats; she knew of an Olympian rower in the next town over whom no inheriting farm boy had ever so much as looked at. All she'd managed was to be known as a very good coach. So, it was no guarantee, but without some sort of feat, it was impossible to make the leap. As she had no skills in painting, Moira put her mind to working on her sports.

On the north edge of town in the shade of the pines, the O'Neals lived in a corrugated-iron-fenced section with mosquitos and magpies and mud. The neighbours said the mother piled car parts into 3-metre-high towers and raged at the wind all through Antarctic storm nights, which was what really split the capillaries all over her nose and cheeks. Though many folk still assumed it was from drink.

Their middle girl, Theresa, with strong thighs and the scent of musk, showed no desire to marry onto a farm, but played all the sports anyway, and on a good day, she impressed, though she was never very consistent. She batted first drop in the summer and, in winter, locked the scrum that, in the winter just gone, had tucked her neatly in behind Moira.

And in this present summer, Moira, who'd had no luck with rugby, was trying her hand at cricket. As luck would have it, the cricket grounds being not far from her house, the country girls would come to her place after school, on account of not having time to get to their own homes and back before Thursday night practice. Theresa would come along too, though she could have made it home first if she'd really tried, due to her both being fast and her home being still in Dregs proper. Though it was on the other side of town.

Apart from Theresa, who would stay mostly quiet when the country girls were there, the girls chattered like brooks on the walk from Moira's to the pitch and Moira felt she was almost at home in this elegant flow. Moira noted their graceful turns of the head and ways of moving not prissy but refined so that she noticed again and again their permanent bracelets of silver and pure Saudi gold, but without their moves ever seeming too flashy. It was the subtlety of it that seemed so like art. Helena Truscott, their opening bat who got her bracelet not till she was six, gushed that Fiona McKercher-Briggs had hers put on when she was a baby, with a tiny insert added each year, lest her small wrist ever be strangled. It made Moira think so differently about her own wrists and what they could be, but when she'd mentioned it to Theresa, after the farm girls had been picked up for home, Theresa said Moira's wrists were fine as they were, and that they didn't have to worry about any of that, anyway. They could have lives away from this. Moira frowned. Theresa would be no help.

Theresa would arrive at Moira's early and would sit on the soft outside couch on the front porch by her window, often arriving before Moira herself in a manner Moira felt was a bit too familiar. She worried the farm girls might think that smell of musk was hers but, being of good manners despite growing up in Dregs proper, she didn't bring it up and of course, being brought up on good farms, nor did they.

On those Thursdays after school that early summer, the farm girls would arrive at Moria's with just the right time left to get to practice, having made the most of getting hot chips in town on the walk to Moira's from school. And, as summer went on, Moira joined them. And pleasure though it was, there was pain with it, too, as week by week the farm girls underwent the dissolving that was known to happen as their inside stuff shifted off to their flash elsewhere schools, where, come February, they would not just attend but live. Even before the end of their last school year all together, and even though they'd still have cricket after the short sports break for Christmas, Moira could start to see the light shine through them when they moved in bright sun. It seemed so unfair, one having only just come to know them, what with them having gone to small far away primaries. But even as the girls started to lose their opacity, their shirts remained present and strong, those fine light shirts of weave that let air breathe through them, in and out and in, so that the girls never showed sweat, even on days that were brutally hot.

Despite her will at improving, and with Theresa's attempts to help with additional practice, Moria never got much better at cricket on account of her shying from that very hard ball as it moved. It's hard to not flinch unless you've grown up with it, the sweet girls from the good farms had said, their voices still resonant with round vowels although their skin by then in January was almost fully transparent. Realising that the wise ghostly girls were likely quite right, even if they were barely here, Moira moved her hopes forward to golf, where she would also have the chance to get to know the mothers of boys who would come to have farms. So, even before the ghost country girls left the cricket team to join the rest of themselves at their new schools at the end of that summer, Moira moved on to golf, and it had felt good to feel herself also dynamic. And being reliably good with mothers and surprisingly so at golf, Moira became something of a darling at the club and the older women praised her swing until she missed a little deliberately, lest she get asked to give lessons and never be seen as the champion amateur she was so determined to be. Theresa, who played the odd round between her team-based pursuits, had spotted Moira's faux missed long drives and had laughed in a way that made Moira feel exposed, as if Theresa didn't care about her one day making it onto a farm at all.

In the late hot days of that summer, Theresa arrived at Moira's anyway one afternoon before cricket, even though Moira had quit some weeks ago now. Moira wondered if Theresa had come to say sorry for laughing, but she didn't say a thing and Moira found other things on her mind. There was her mother's new baby to care for and then the number 8 wire fencing knot she'd been working on and that she'd been thinking to enter in the women's auxiliary trials. So, she went back inside to the baby and to sketch out her plans for future prize-winning fences and didn't think about Theresa again.

Back out the front, the evening came on very warm, and in the morning, Theresa wasn't there, neither on the couch nor anywhere in Dregs, not as far as anyone could tell. Her musk, though, remained, melted down into the couch mixed with the polyester cotton blend, a scent that persisted, so that no matter how hard anyone scrubbed, in the end, it had to be burned.

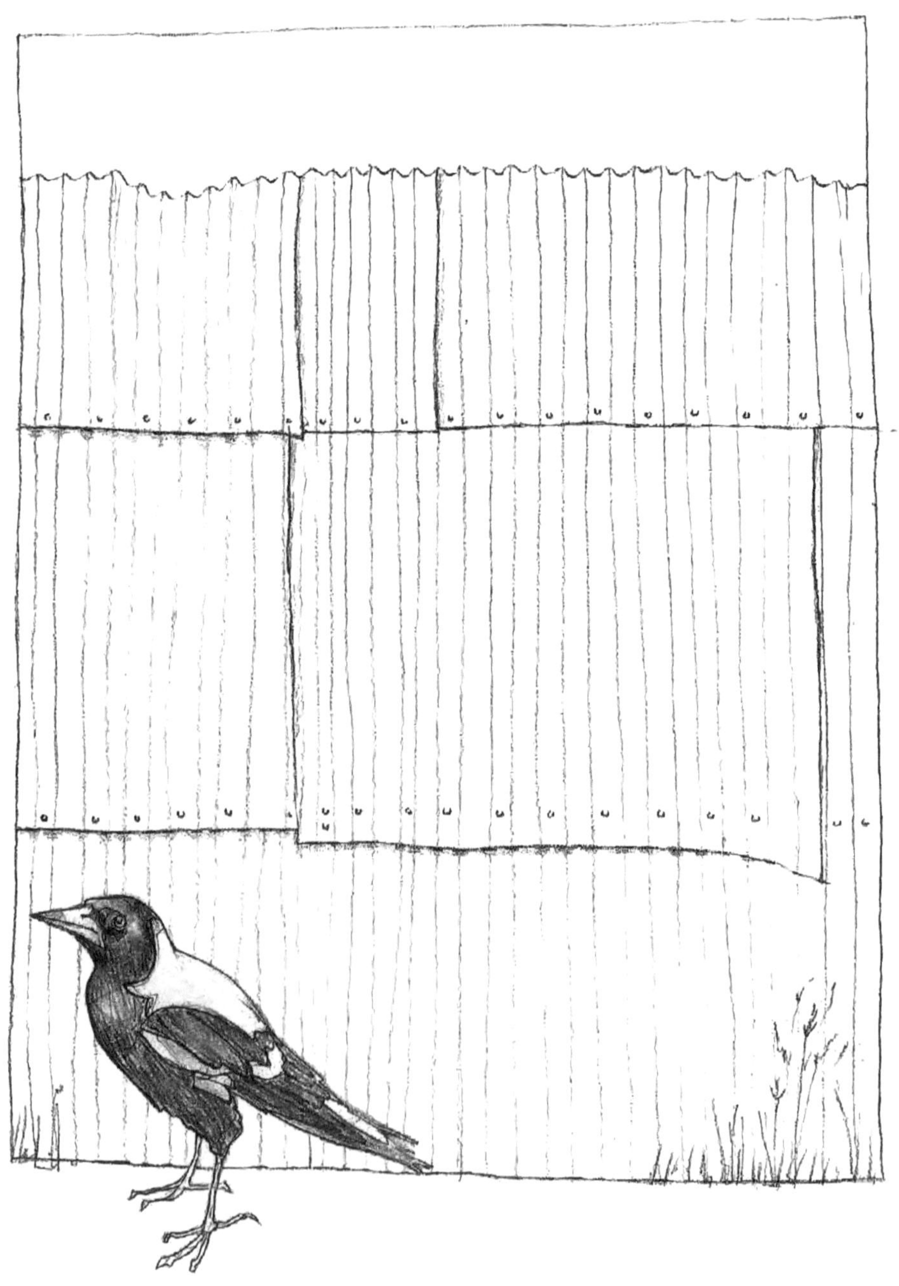

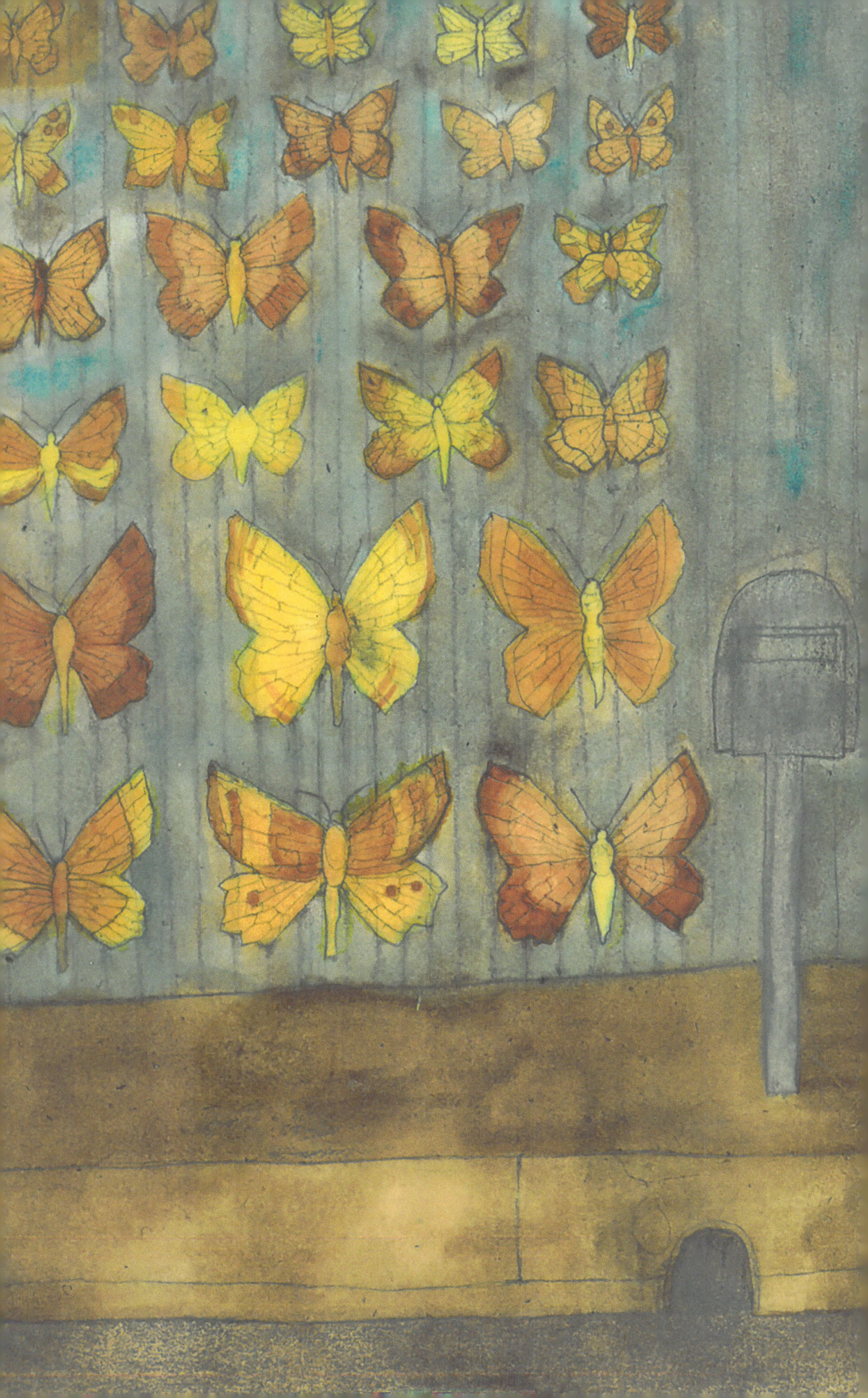

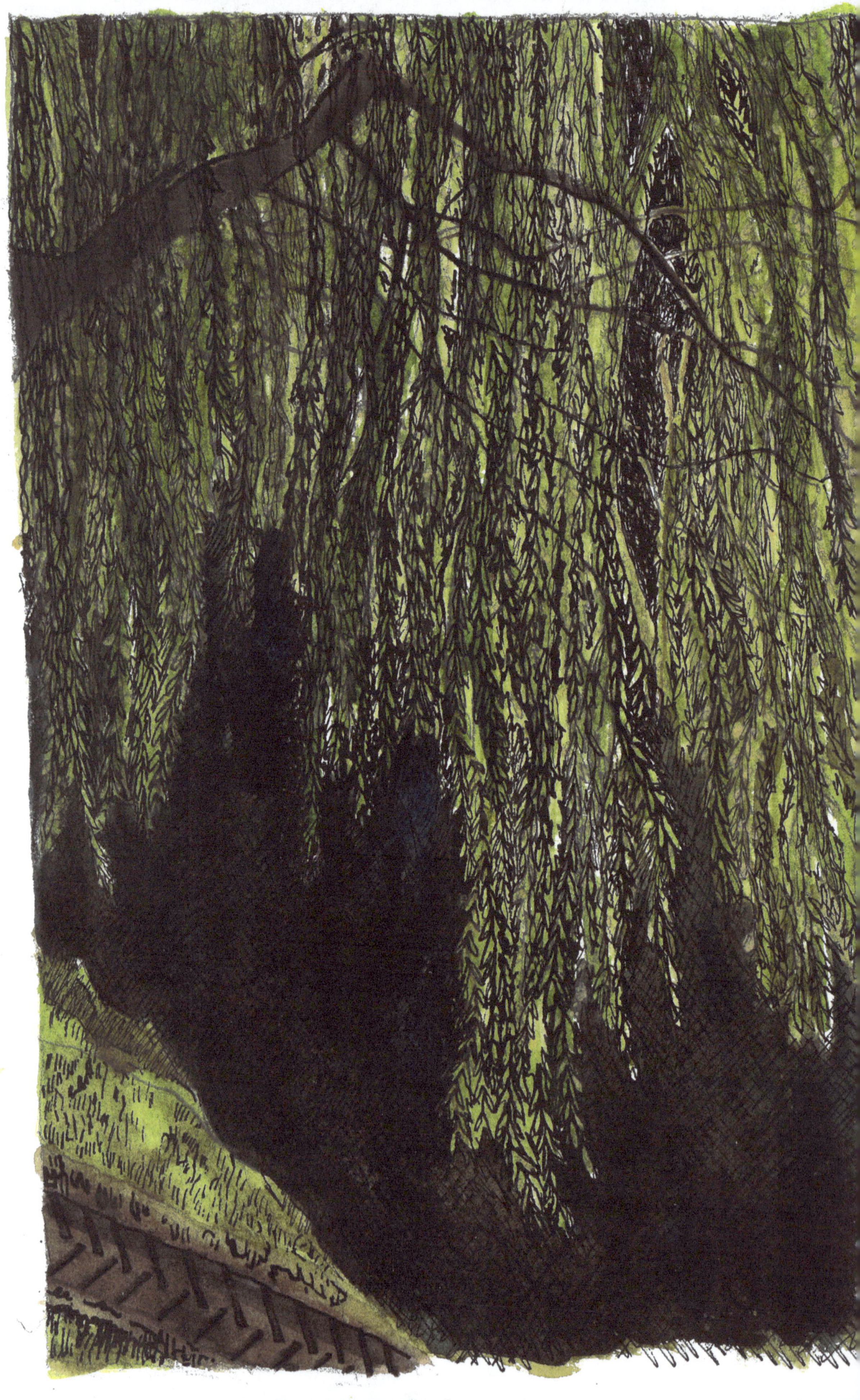

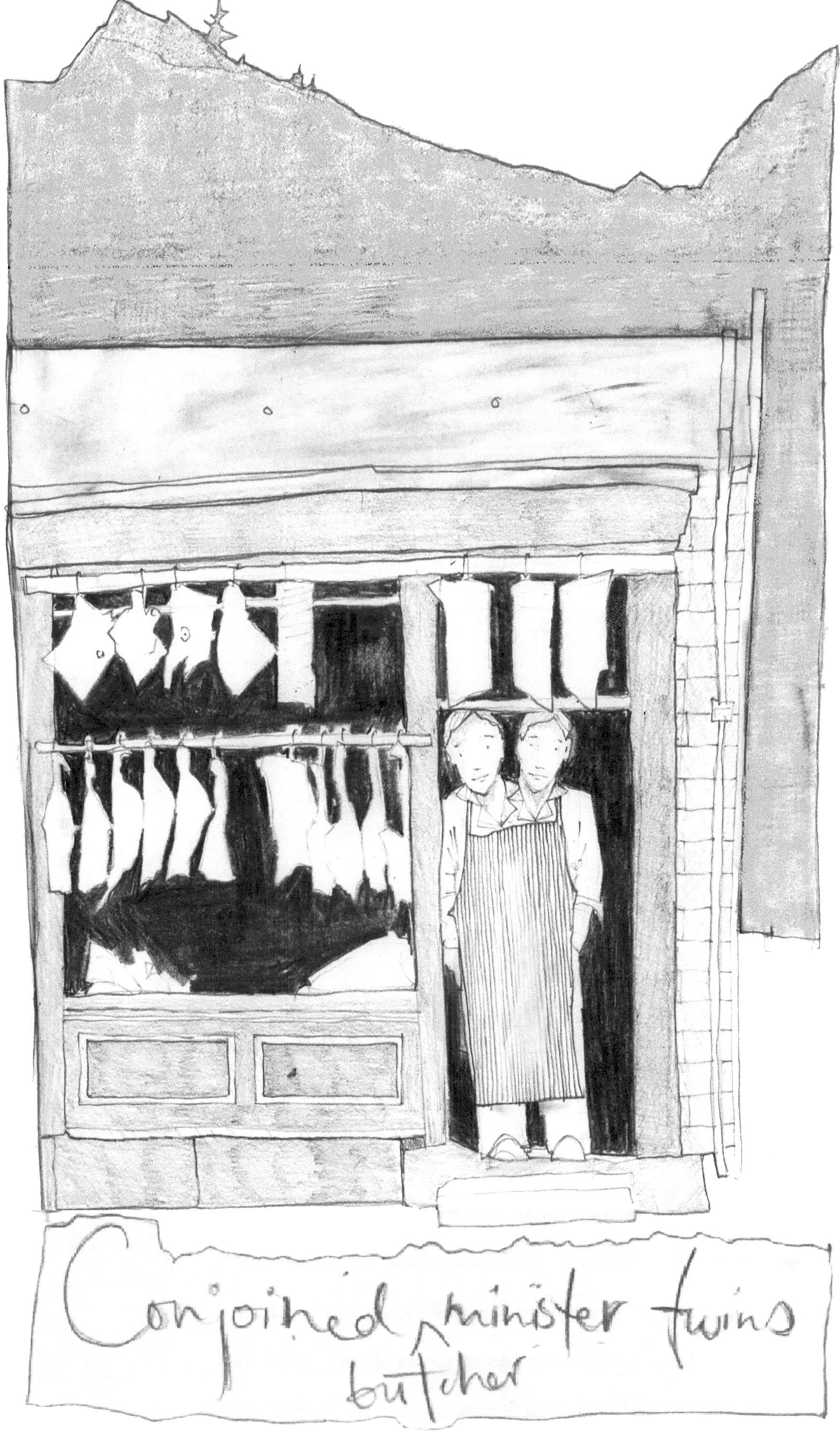

Conjoined minister twins
butcher

After the first of many downturns, the post office in Dregs folded into the bookshop, which, in turn, was run through the bank, which itself had gone part-time, so that tellers picked up caregiving work from the recently closed old folk's home (although this work would soon be made unpaid). The lay ministry lost its stipend, so the manse was set up to sell knick-knacks to tour groups who passed through from June to October, heading up to ski fields where the snow falls white and stays that way. Knick-knack sales paid for church morning teas and the flowers and repairs, though lay ministers had to find their own homes.

Mick lay-preached the first fortnight of each month and Henry the second. They butchered together and shared a sweet little wife that they loved together but never at the same time. For decency, one would cover himself with the family's Indian print duvet and think on the word of the Lord, drinking His wisdom, while the other would fill up their little wife, with her skin smoother than possibility (but for her hands, which were worked rough as anyone's). And the suffering the duvet-covered husband must have felt! But they were true men of God, those two, and they prayed and it all worked okay.

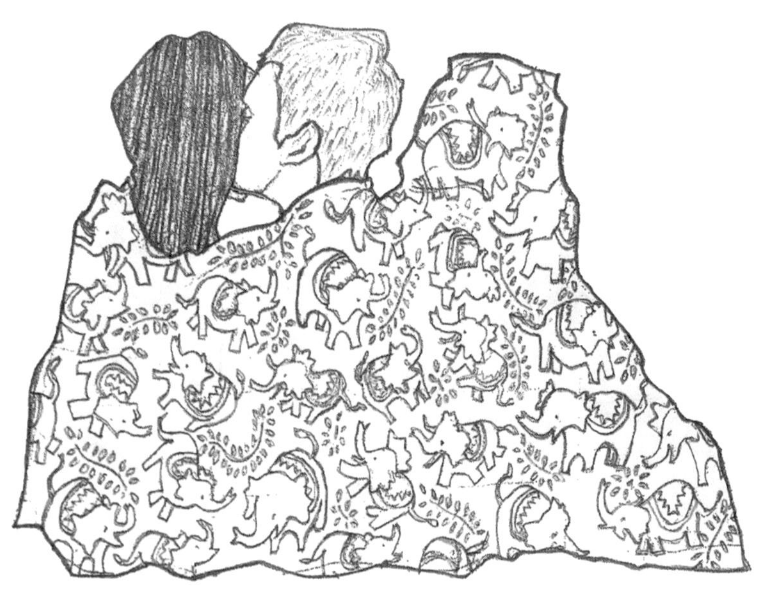

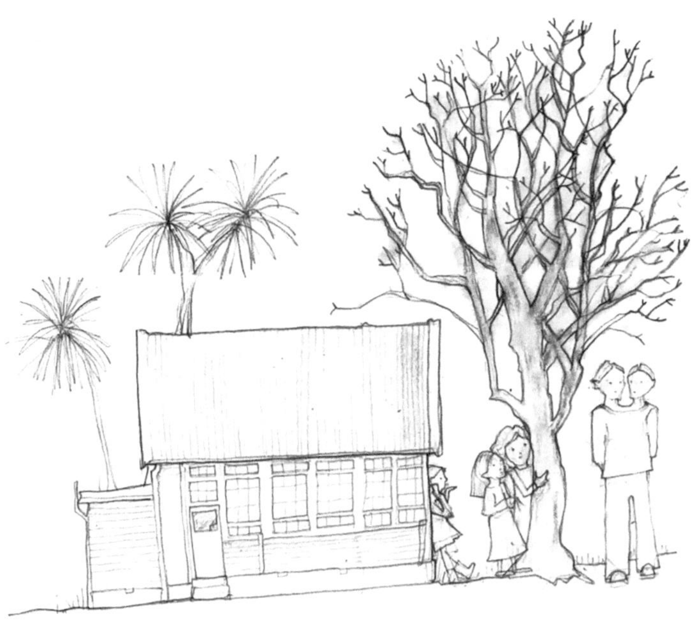

At Western Dip Primary (before it was closed and the kids out there had to travel into Dregs proper for school each day), long before the twins found their little wife and took up gloves in public, their hands loomed large in the classroom. Hands of aching mass, already worn and thick, but with thumbs as sensitive as anything. Back at school, you could imagine those hands pressing right up against your crotch, and when it all became too much, they would know and flatten their palms to your bliss and no girl could focus on her maths. It was a wonder anyone passed at all. Red socks flashed under their trousers and made you wonder if those two would dance at home with their love when they found her. But they were godly boys even then, and girls hung their heads at what they'd imagined. At the end of it all, when they had to choose a wife, everyone knew it would only be one for the two of them and they didn't choose you, or Helena, or Cindy, who was surely captivating enough for anyone, or so anyone would have thought, but the girl who was so quiet and fine that no-one had known her name. But if you'd noticed her, you'd have wondered about touching her skin, and it would have been torture, that wonder.

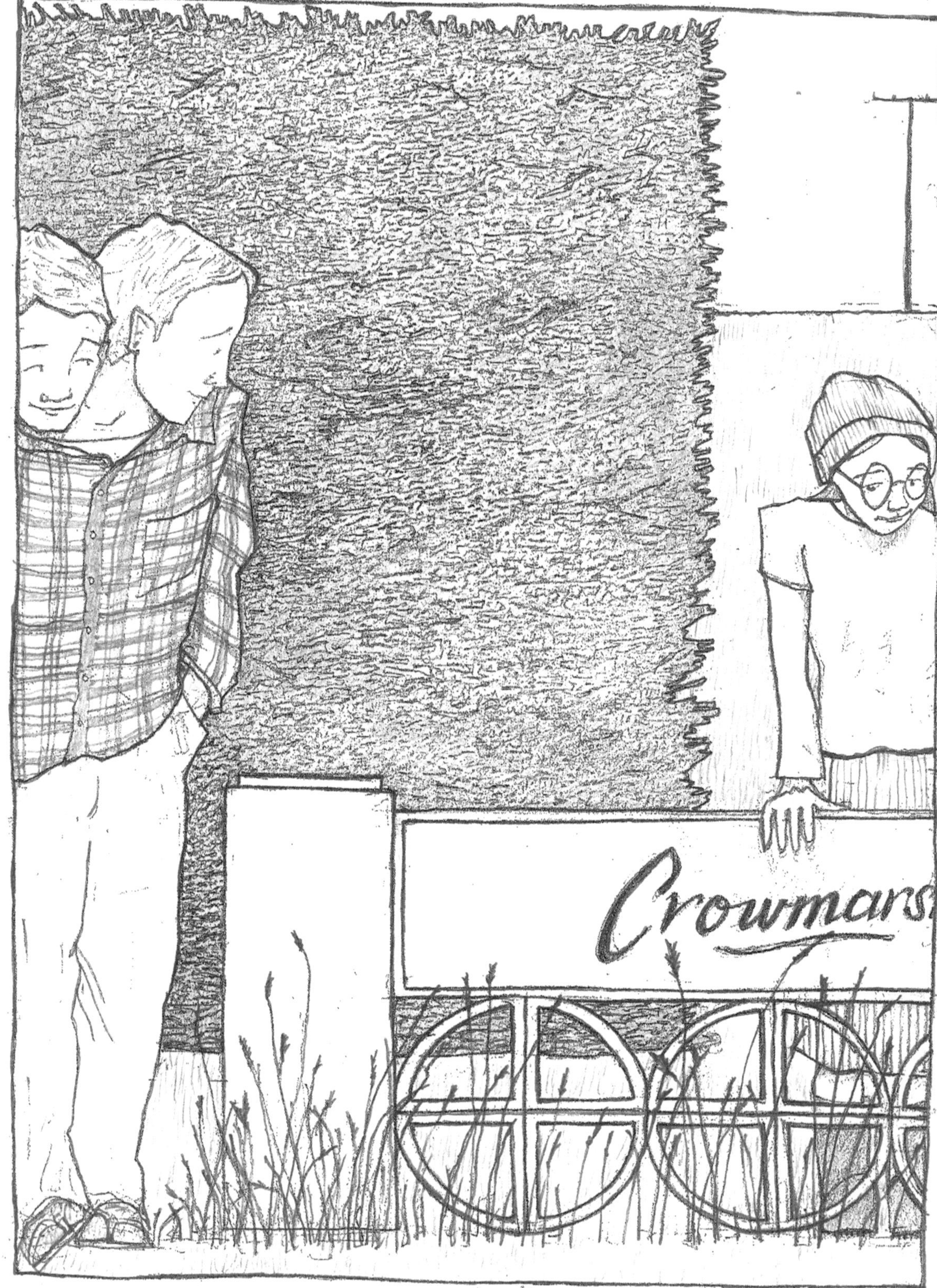
Crowmans

Dregs Women's Hospital was long closed by that stage, and after the vet picked up the blacksmithing she couldn't help at the simple births like she had, not even on a Sunday. By then, even the pharmacist, who from necessity had long given more advice than he possibly should have, was rarely to be found, having gained work in Temuka after Mrs McCaskill bought the chemist shop and converted it for garden ornaments.
She'd hardly sold a thing, the wares being so expensive, but that wasn't the point, she'd said, and Mr McCaskill agreed. So, when it came to birthing, most local women went out to Timaru the week before they were due so their babies could be caught out there in the pale green and the Dettol. But for that you need a driver, and the little wife kept to herself (which isn't praise in these parts), so she brought her babies herself at home, sluicing off the blood and mucus with the fine culinary hose (more gentle than you'd think) that her husbands had brought her from work. And each winter she delivered them children, squeezed from her surprisingly robust tiny frame, clean by the time the husbands returned. Eleven in all and not a pair of them joined up. The husbands would hold their resourceful little wife. Our dear little brave little love.

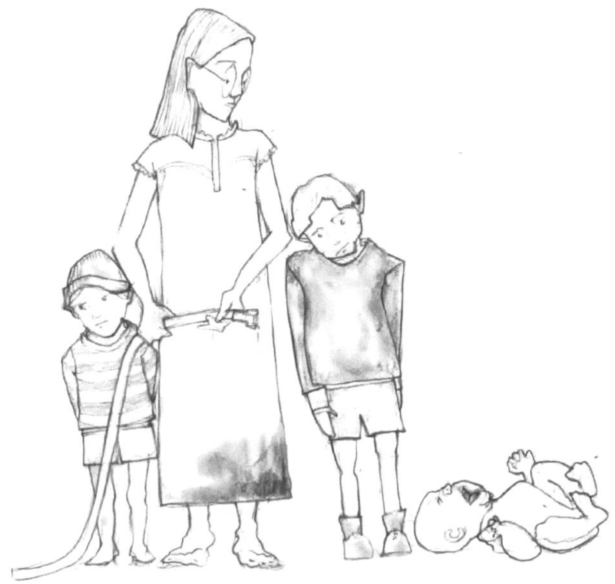

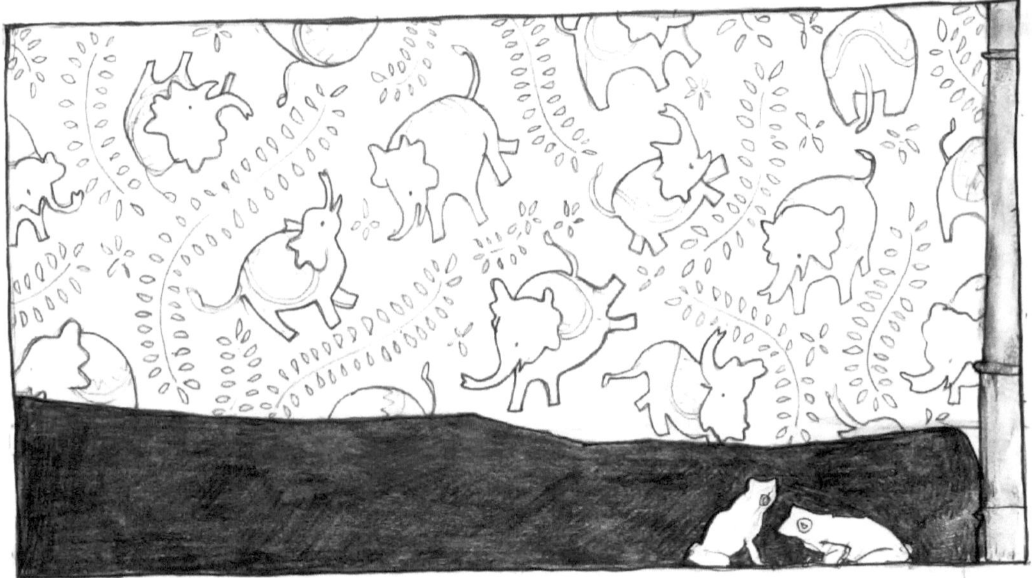

And which husband fathered whom wasn't a matter; Joseph never quibbled
fatherhood (not after Gabriel had explained). The kids were as sweet as you
could wish, but who wouldn't be, growing up as they did with their fathers
at home every night and the hum of their parents' loving streaming through
the house, leaving it moist and warm. Young brown tree frogs left their
tarns for the home's damp corners and drowned in the clemency there.
In the evenings, wives trying for children crept up to bathe in the light of
the place.

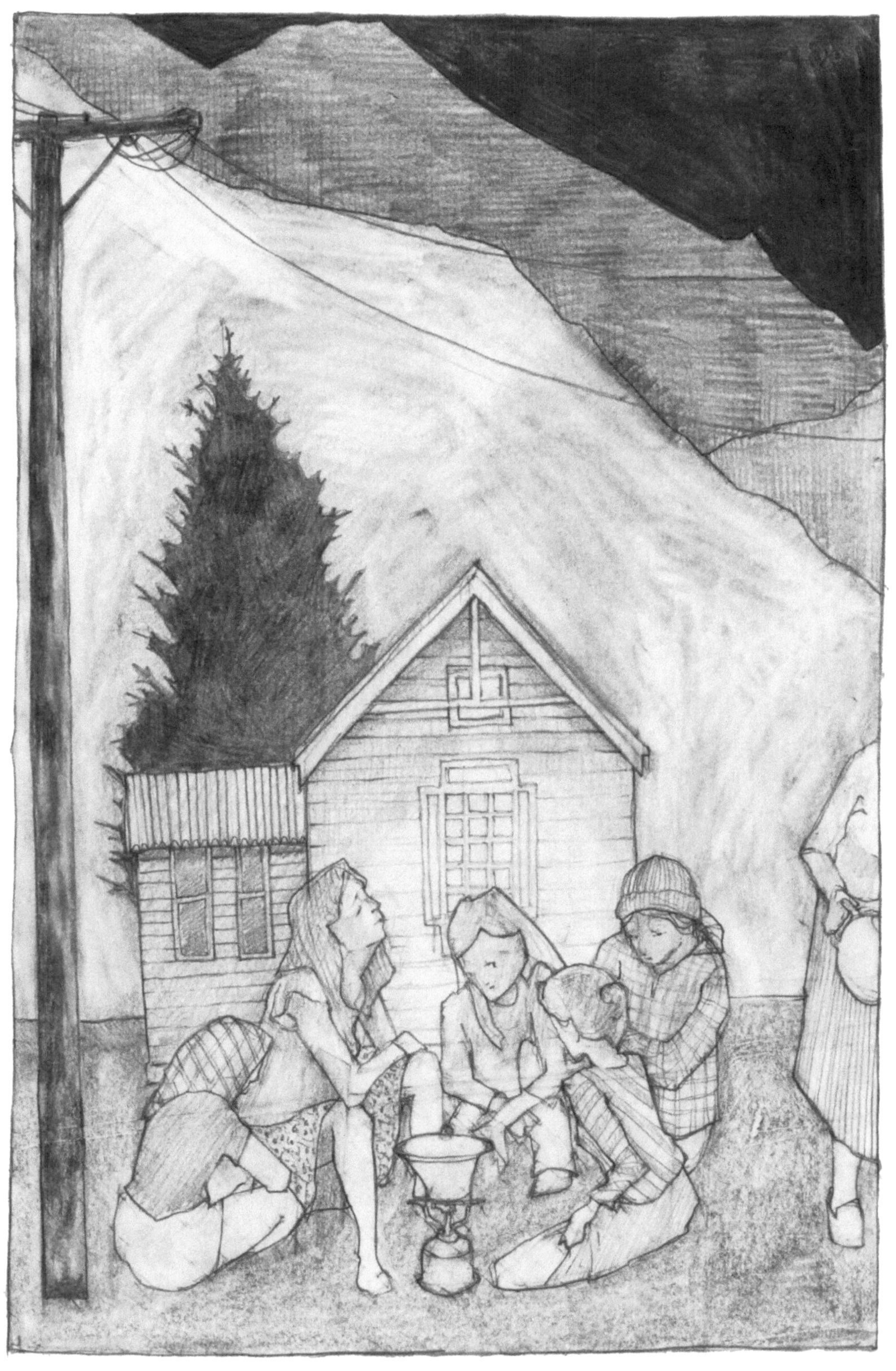

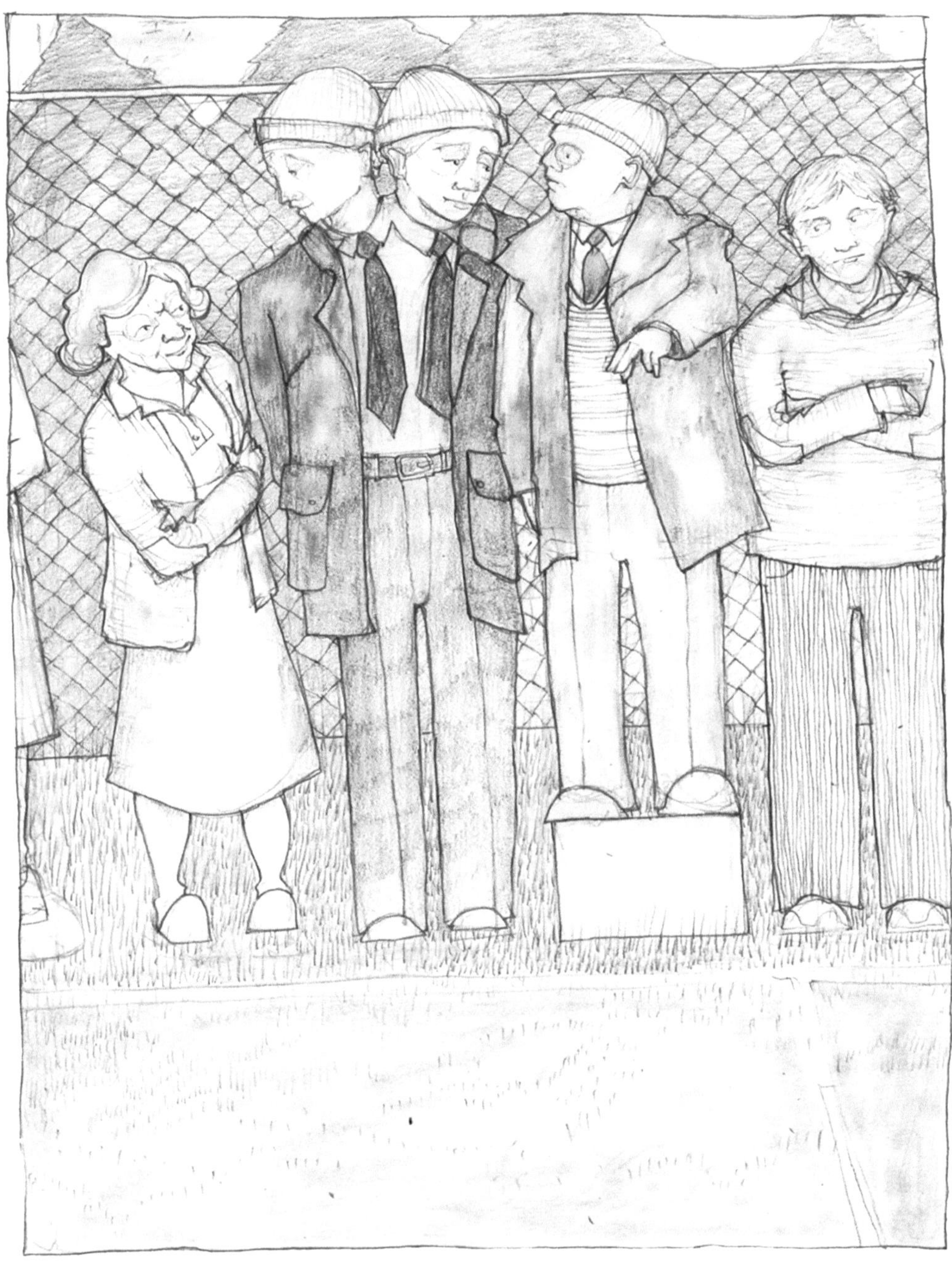

During the day, the fathers, by necessity, were gone. Sundays they preached. Weekdays they butchered, with unpaid lunchtime Trust decisions, council clean-ups and fire brigade call-outs. There were apprentices to coach and unfortunates' foundations to re-pile. Saturdays they watched rugby at the Domain, but didn't play, as it's forbidden for dicephalous parapagus twins, even if they are highly symmetric and in remarkable health. The children stayed at home and embraced their warm little mother.

And they touched her with their soft children's hands that don't mind to touch you, even when you're old and so rough from work it's a wonder their soft pink skins aren't flayed off as they stroke. But their warm flesh remained, and they stroked. The boys lingered in their touching and had their fine mother hide under their little arms to protect her from the stranger in the van parked out east or from the ghost of Tall Frederick who was still trying to find whomever killed his eels. Soft in the warmth of their underarms, their little mother would forget about the library position going over in Dregs proper where she'd heard they'd lately taken to closing off traffic and dancing in great lines in the middle of the street on a Thursday. Her girls pawed at her, fleeting and exact, and she shivered a gentle revulsion. But God flowed through her, as through all His children. So she opened her pores to His will and gave suck to the daughters too, though in time, Praise Be, they would grow away from her to cry out for kittens. And when the kittens came, they would stroke them gently, loving them on to their small pink nipples. It wasn't right, she would say when she saw it, sweet girls don't put cats to their breasts. But when the little mother would finally turn her head, the girls, it seemed, couldn't help themselves. Blood seeped into the carpet.

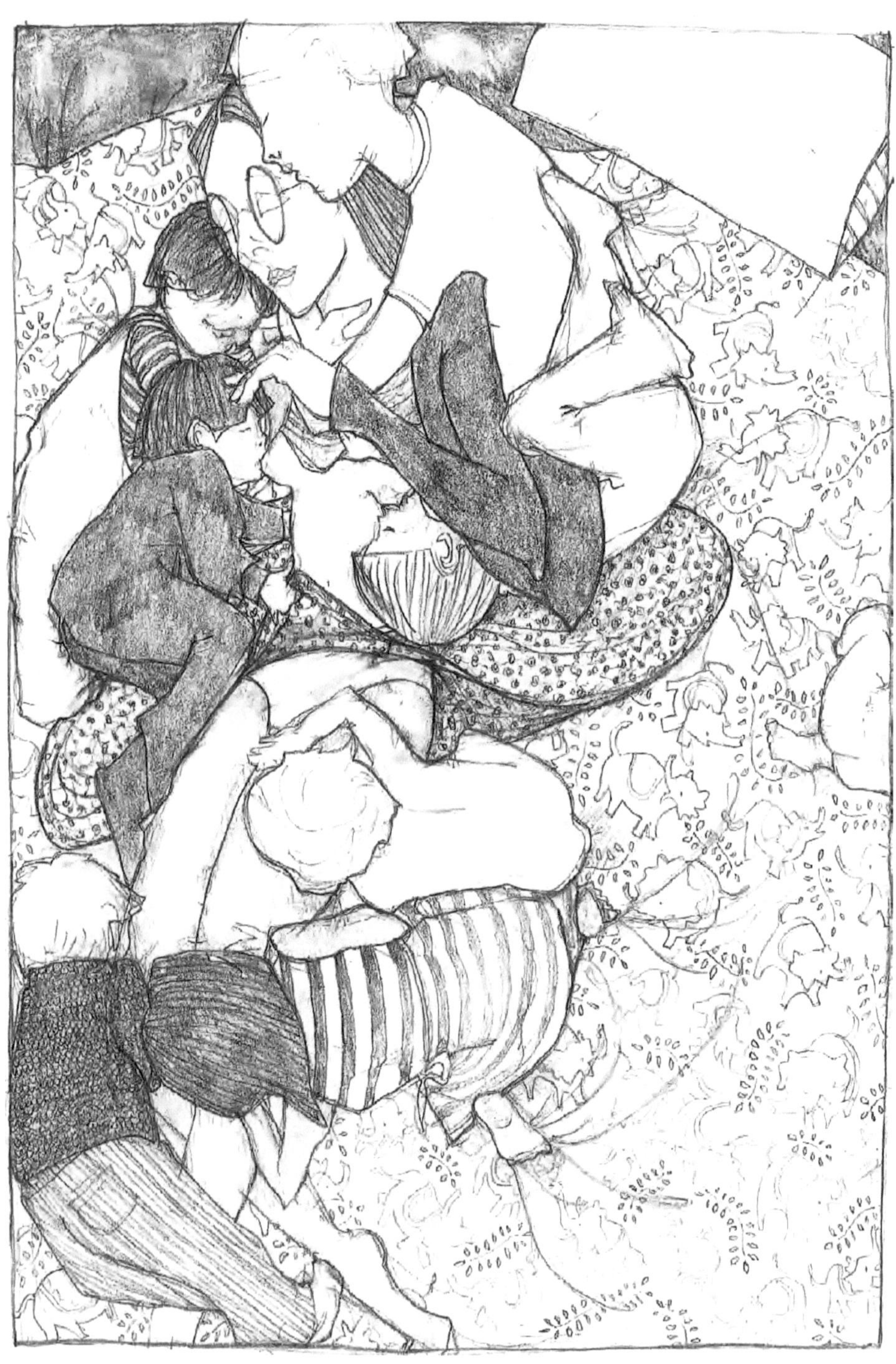

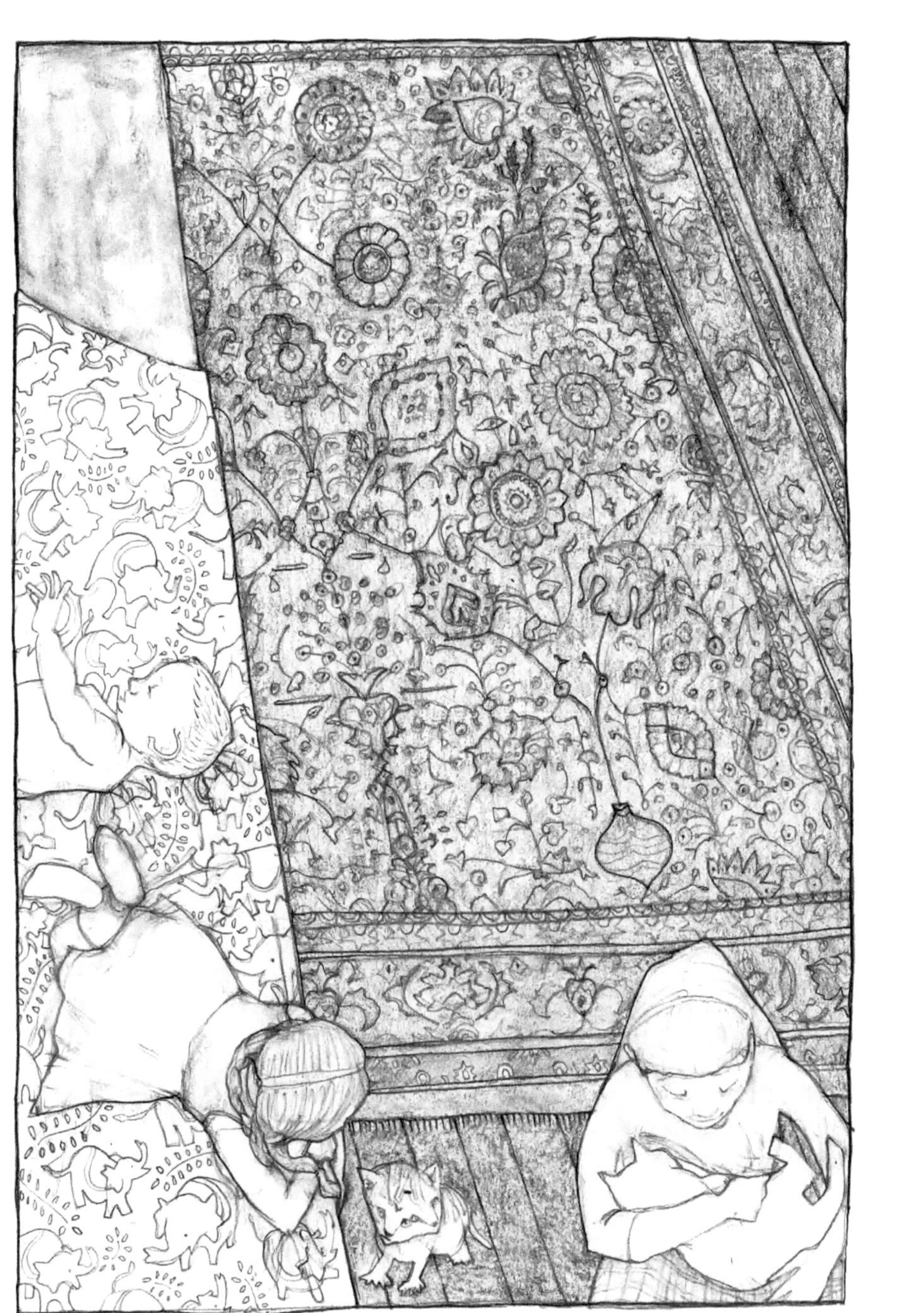

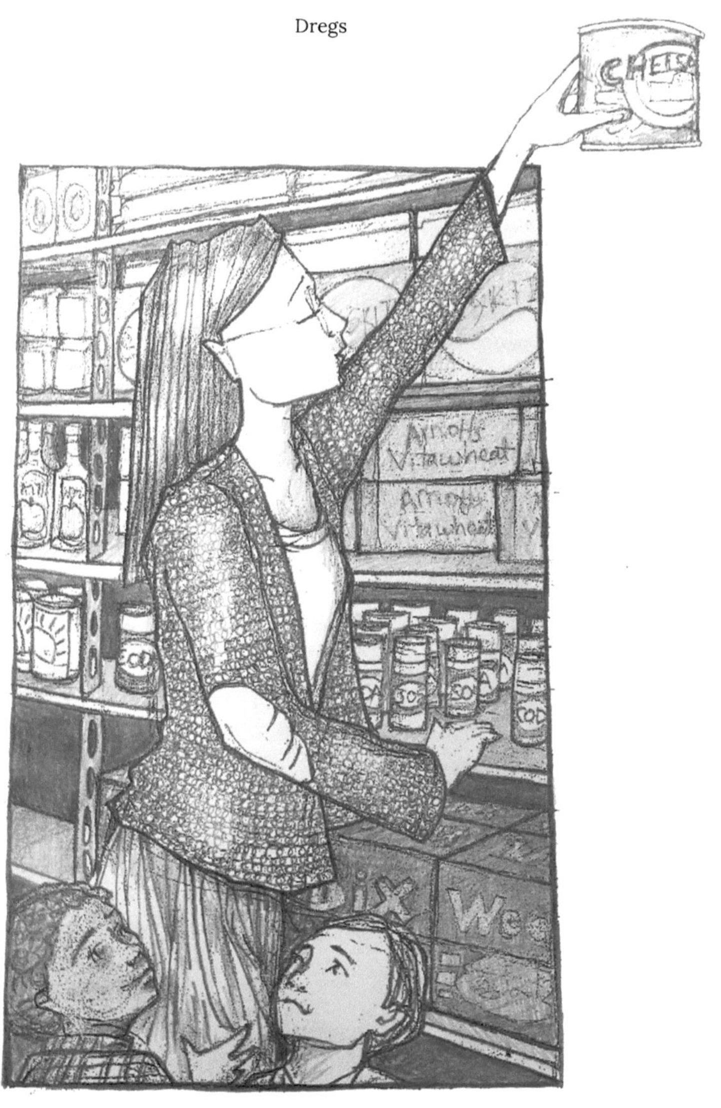

Attended by her boys, who wouldn't let her out of their sight, she walked
to get food for her young, growing, brood. The little wife's husbands
were never home until much later, on account of them having to take up
Mulvihill's Fish Monger and Chips (with a side trade in small plastic snakes
and yoyos) to help keep the butchery afloat. So the little wife could take
time with her shopping although, on account of Thompson's Bakery and
Nicholson's Greengrocers collapsing into Sheriff's SuperValue, she was
mostly shopping all at one place. A little hand took hers as she walked back
down the aisle for molasses. A thumb moved in firm circles on her palm. A
son's warm forearm brushed her calf as he picked up the wholemeal flour
at her feet. The boys made deals among themselves to travel beneath her
pleated skirt and encourage her as she went, so gracefully, about her day. A
little son licked the golden syrup that had almost crept to the bottom of the
tin. They all watched for future slips that might threaten the tin's paper-
wrapped neighbours (Dear little eagle-eyed loves).

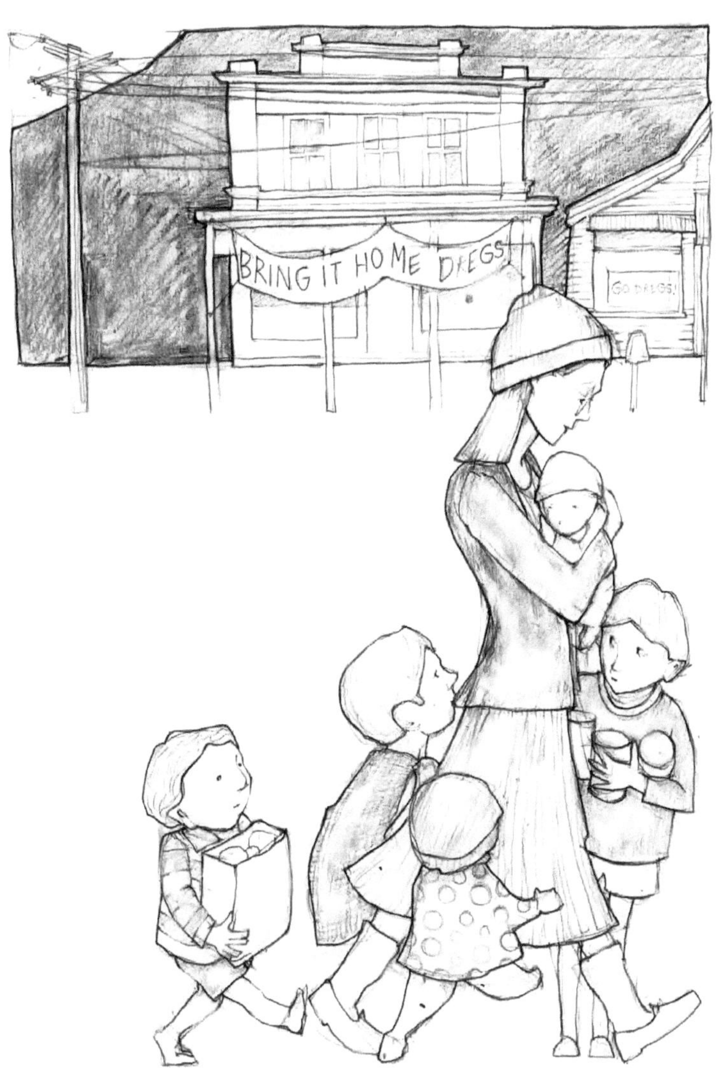

BRING IT HOME DREGS
GO DREGS!

The butchery soon incorporated the hardware aisle of Harris's, so the husbands were very busy and could no longer get home for tea. The little wife could walk the long way home and still be back in time for their later arrivals back home (though she had to walk the long way regardless on account of the old Village Green shortcut being blocked by the Royal Hotel extension). On Thursdays she ate secret canned salmon by the river with her boys and, at home, the girls foraged mushrooms for tea.

Book troubles meant Maling's Toy & Shoe Shop was no longer self-supporting and was forced under the management of Grantham's Haberdashers, which had already taken over the uniformers, along with the liability for the red school jerseys that just wouldn't sell. The old shell of Mailing's reopened as a food stop for passing-through skiers run by people no-one here knew or would ever really come to. But the new place gave vouchers for free meals to local shop owners, who mostly now didn't get home for lunch, so no-one said too much about the change. The Lions went into recession and the management of the volunteer fire brigade lost its funding, so the butchers had to take it on, along with all the rest. They found they didn't have time anymore to walk home each night and so took to sleeping in turn, while standing, so that one could always work. They would grab breakfast on the job.

Though it would just be until things picked up.

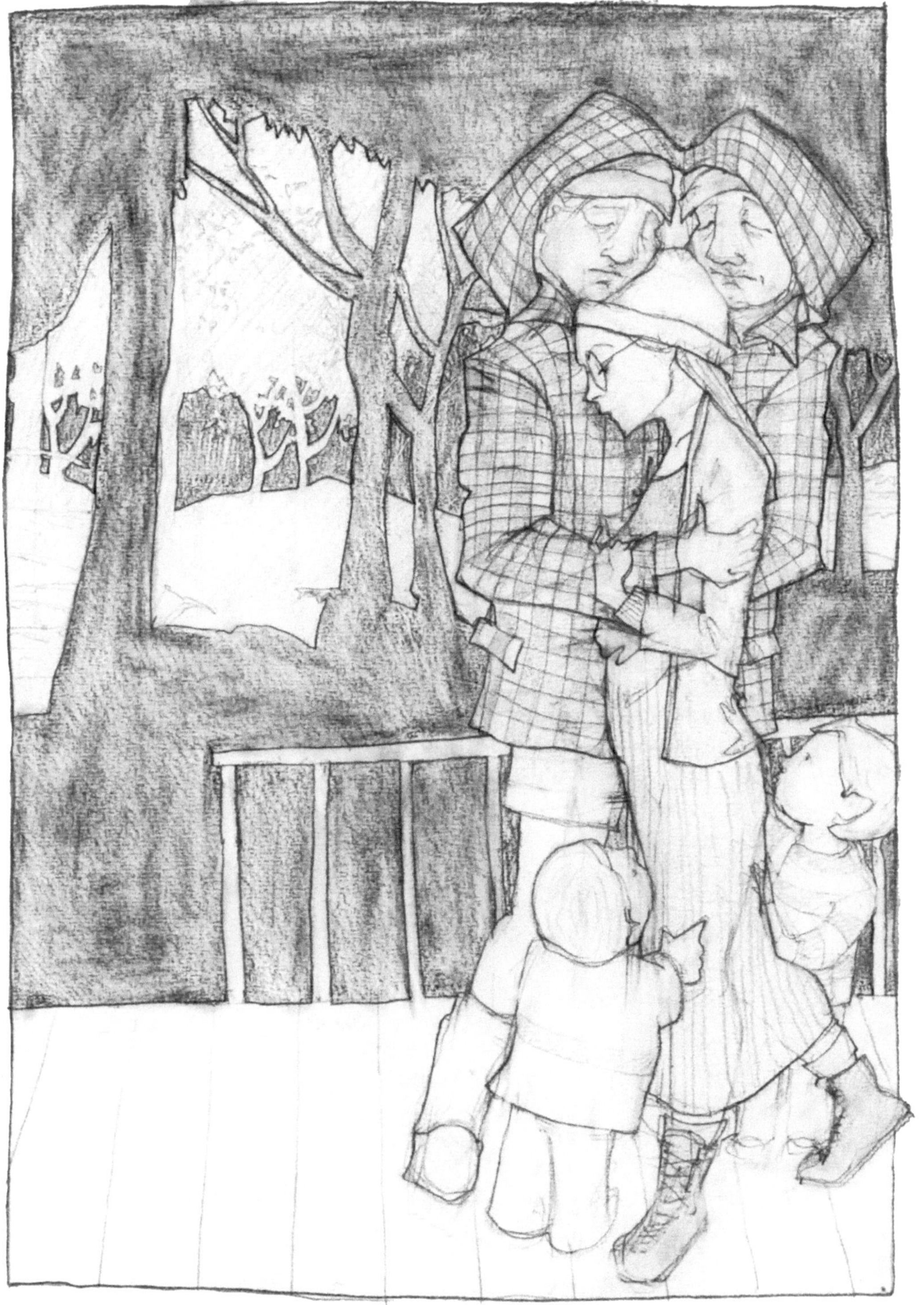

With her husbands not coming home even for breakfast or love, there was nothing for the little wife to do but send her girls off, there no longer being a father around to protect them. Of course, they were all snapped up as soon as you could wish, being beautiful girls like their mum. And all were well-loved, as their mother had been. And her boys were hardworking like their dads, and loyal good helps around home.

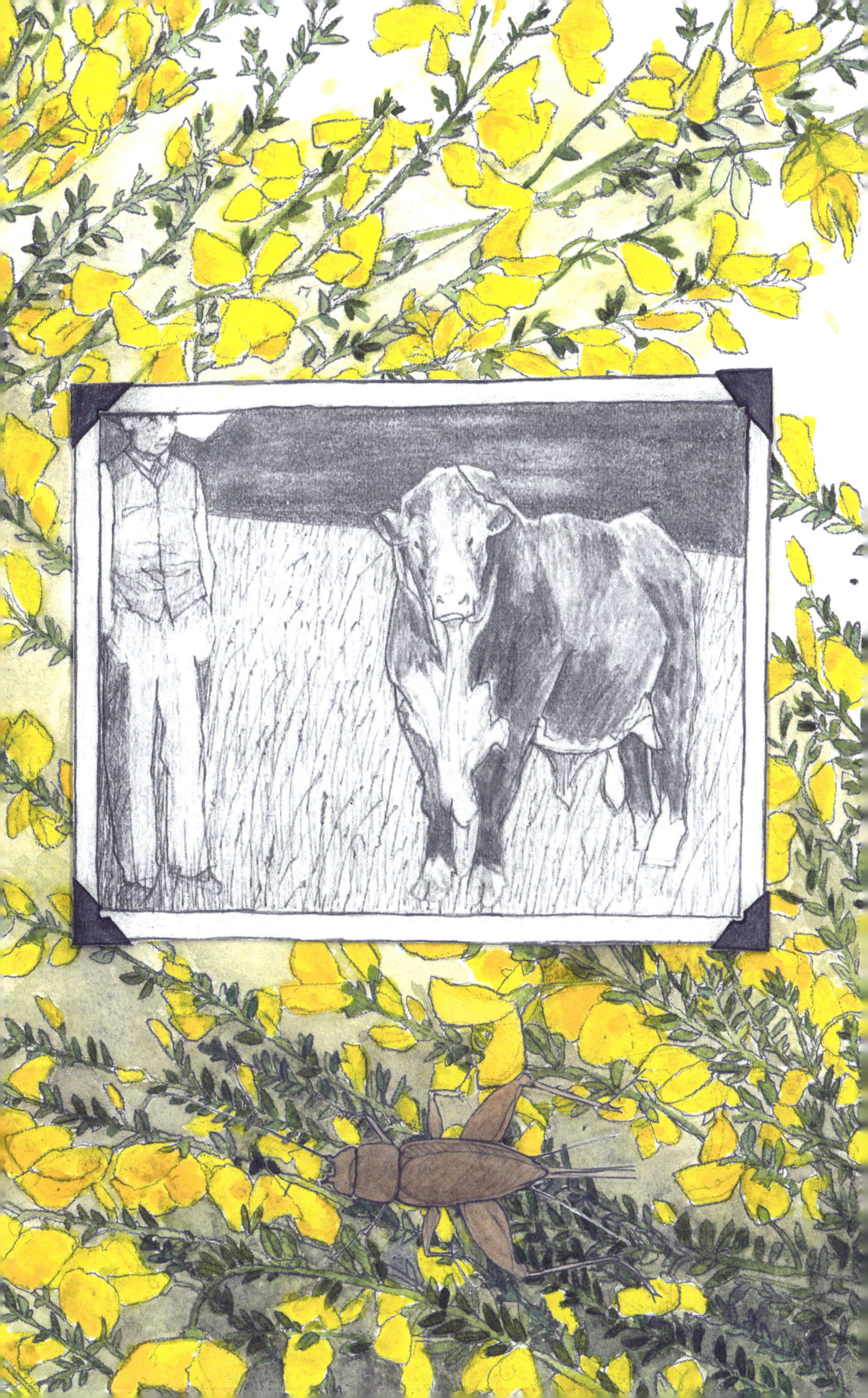

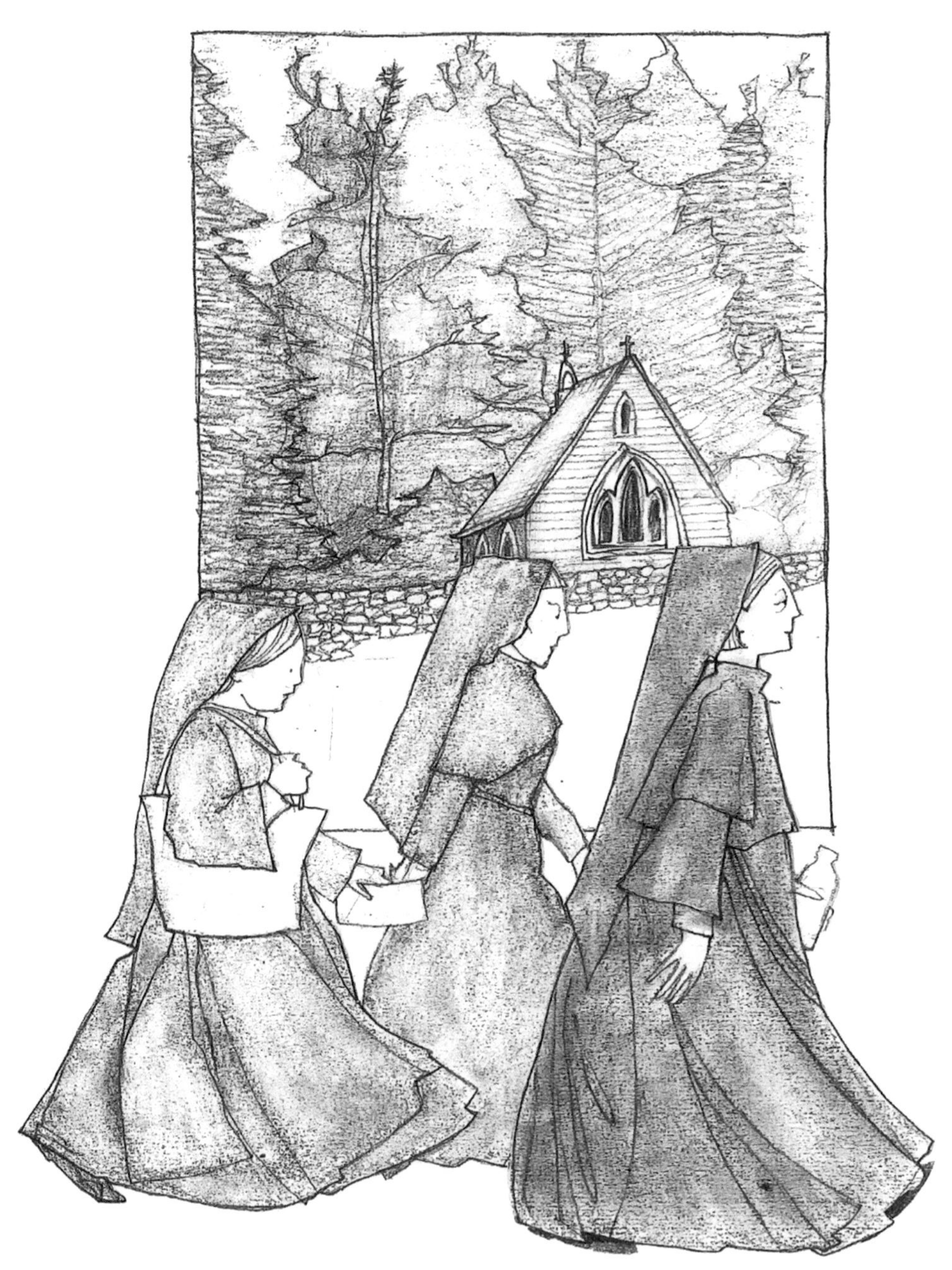

Walter Clift

After a while, Walter had seen too much death. The Robinsons had left for Oamaru, as God had said plainly there was a cloud coming for men. Or, really, for boys. For those on the cusp. They'd told only the Chisholm-McLennans who, being progressive types down from the city, had known better than to take this odd prophecy for truth but, being tolerant of quaint beliefs, made warm sounds and had nodded quite gravely before offering another round of tea and asking about soccer teams for the boys down in Oamaru. But, as unlikely as it had sounded, the cloud had come.

Close to a death a year had come, for some years now. Despite his old-sounding name (a product of his not-from-here mum), Walter was young and kept his shirt buttoned up against the cloud, though he'd had some protection anyway, with a mother not from anywhere speaking English, which sociologists would later confirm as protective but which even then we'd suspected.

Though he himself would make it through, still each death had rent something, both within him and without, weakening the pull that held the tomatoes in time, and that kept baby kokopu wanting both the sea and return. Even the deaths of boys he'd been scared of, popular boys whose humour had thrived on slivers of viciousness, had left him unsure how to move through the day. But some had plain ripped him in two. He still missed Hamish Evans, though they'd never been friends in earnest. They'd learned to juggle by the back-school chestnut tree in that final week of the year when people's guards were down on account of the long summer break almost being here. Having played soccer due to his not-from-here mum, he'd never known that rugby boys could be so gentle. That week, he and Hamish had worked up to keeping four batons in the air all at once and had coordinated a little accompanying dance. A double left step, a right, and a bow.

And now, though he wasn't any longer at school, it was still going on, and with he and Ruthie planning kids of their own, it was hard to know what to do.

When he was younger, back before the deaths and deaths, he'd found grey-and-fawn-coloured creatures inside him with not enough hair to call fur, little beings somehow always quite clammy, damp even in the cold and the dry. He'd pulled them out, one by one, them seeming like something to pluck rather than keep. He hadn't minded so much at the time that less feeling came through from where he'd made the extractions. Alongside the slight numbing, he found himself longing for anything sweet and became known for his baking and roundness and people said no-one would love him on account of it but Ruthie had, fiercely.

Somehow now, all these years later, thinking of the babies he and Ruthie hoped to have took him down to the creek and, somehow, those creatures still waited, shining clammy through the sparseness of their hair but somehow more handsome for their time in the mud. He'd checked and no-one was looking and, at an urge, he'd kissed each one full on the lips and there in the mud of the creek they'd each flashed golden before passing into his chest, which grew so reassuringly warm he didn't care who might have seen. And he'd laughed.

And he remembered Ruthie talking about the uses of watercress and that he'd wanted to add some to a pie, so he gathered a sap green bundle and one sprig of cherry blossom for his buttonhole and another for Ruthie's blouse. The pink of the blossom caught the late afternoon light and he'd cried a little and hadn't known why, but when he moved his spine was fluid like the short-tailed cats he and Ruthie had seen on TV just last week, and the heel-toe, heel-toe of his feet on the earth lit a private smile that glowed down through his belly to his knees and into the soil.

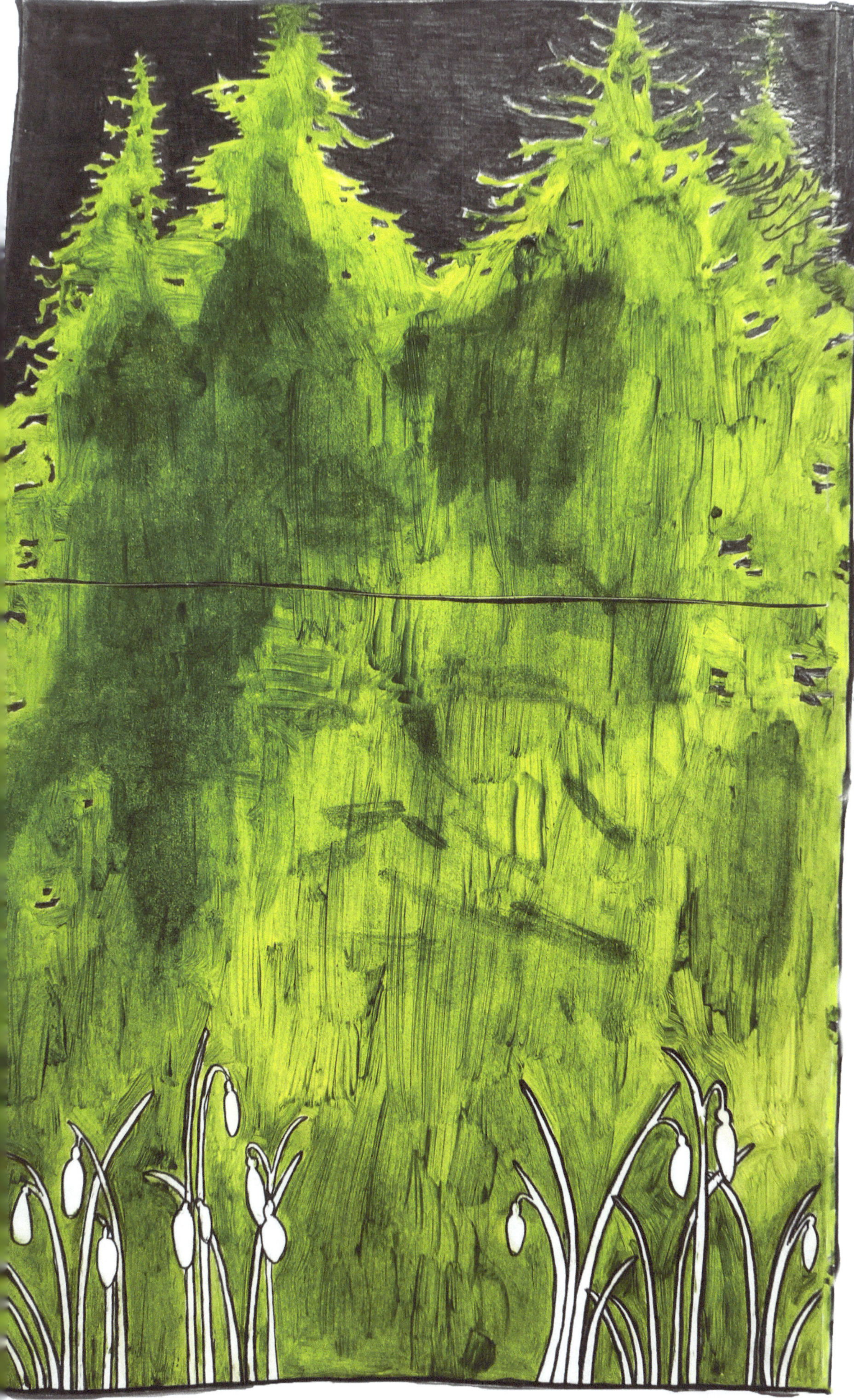

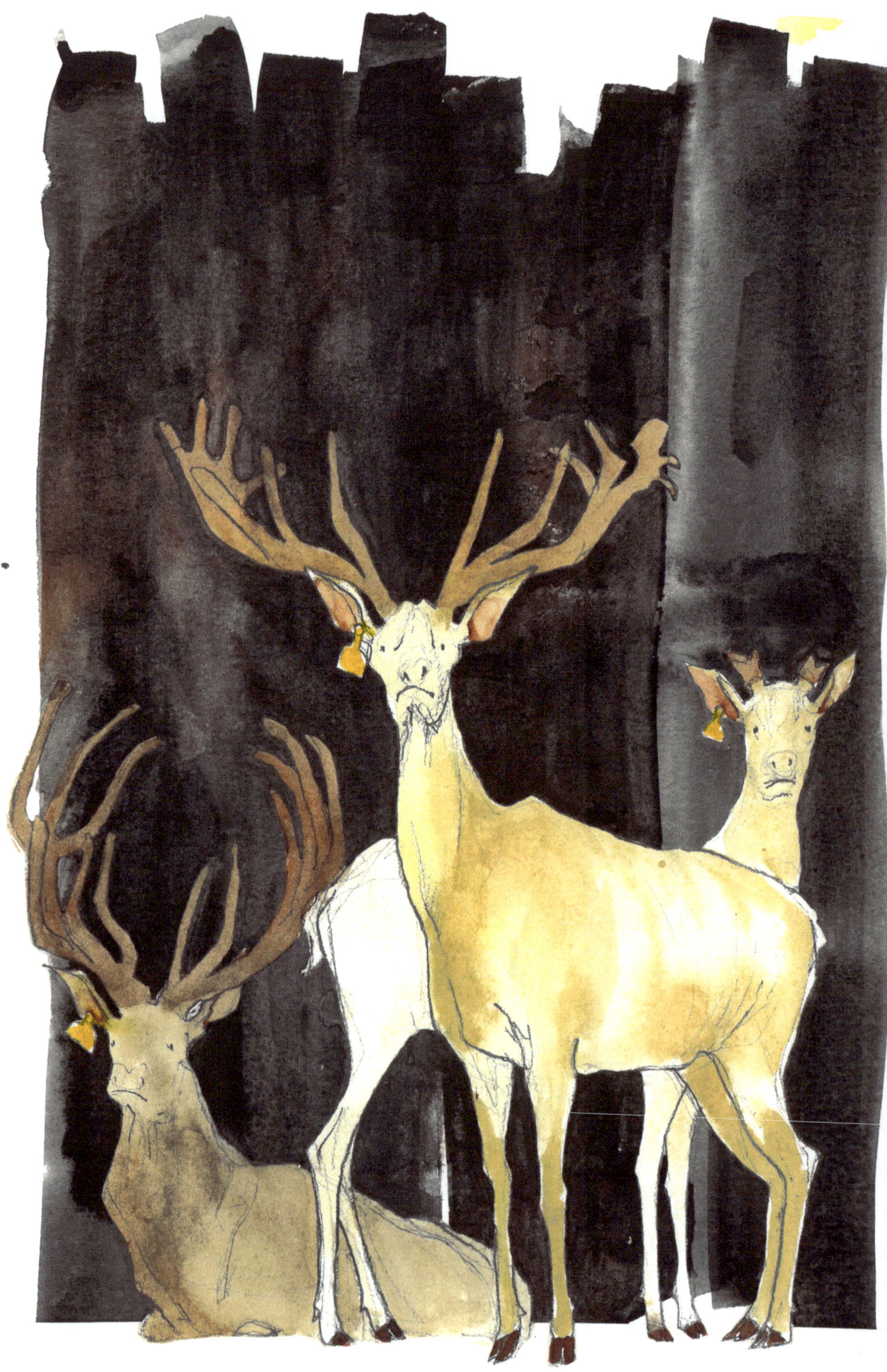

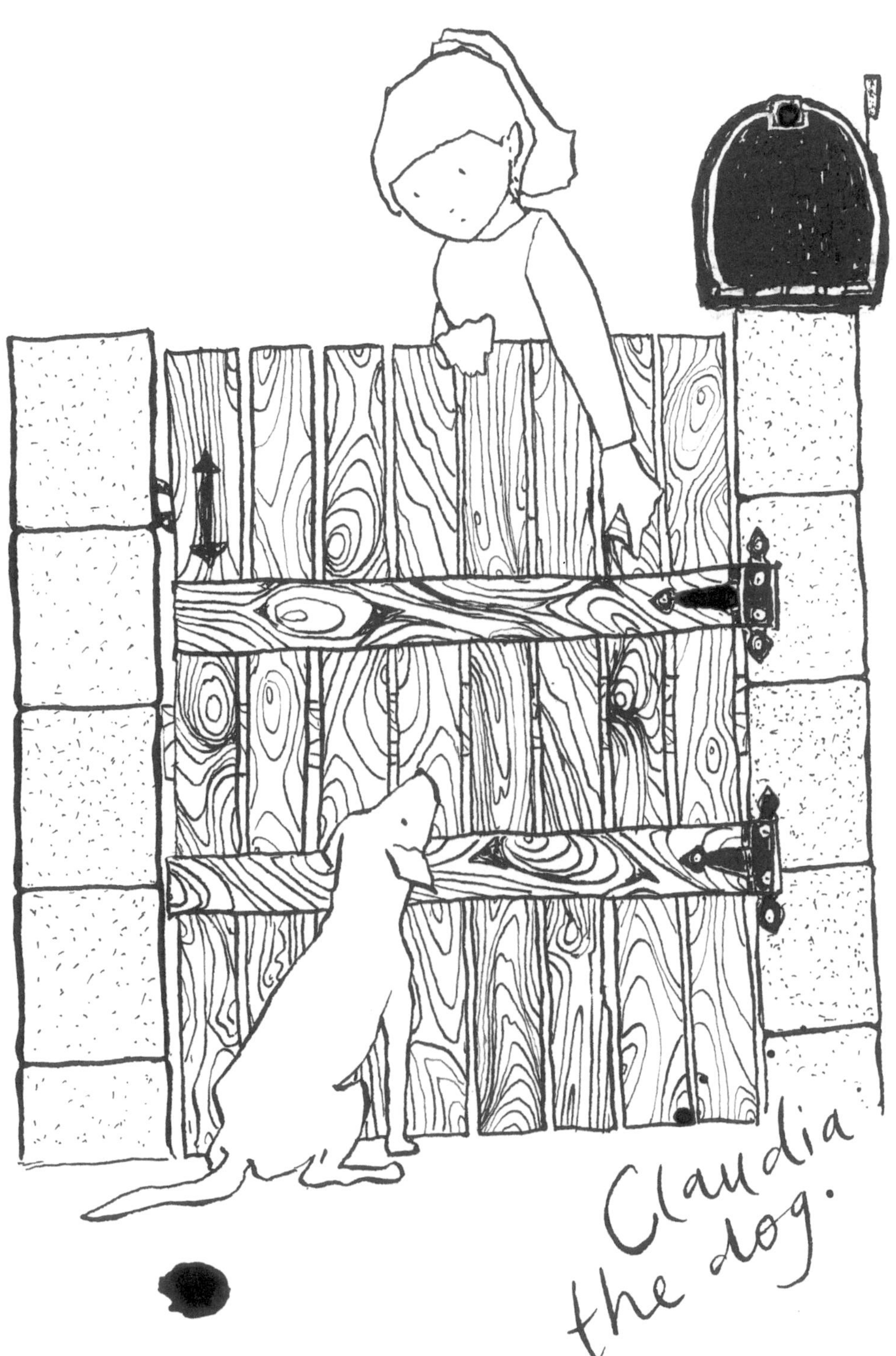

Claudia
the dog.

The Granthams arrived in Dregs from out of town and hadn't known about
the time Pete Truscott threw himself down his offal pit after he found
Little Ted, his working huntaway, strung up on the new electric fencing.
Or when Chris Ellery was sent to Cherry Farm for arranging a wedding for
him and Sweet Chrissy who, it must be said, was fine and yellow and kind.
Chris wasn't right, even after he came back, and now lives out East, where
no-one bothers with weddings. The Granthams hadn't known about the
trouble that comes with getting too close to your dogs. They gave their dog
a people name, and the trouble started from there.

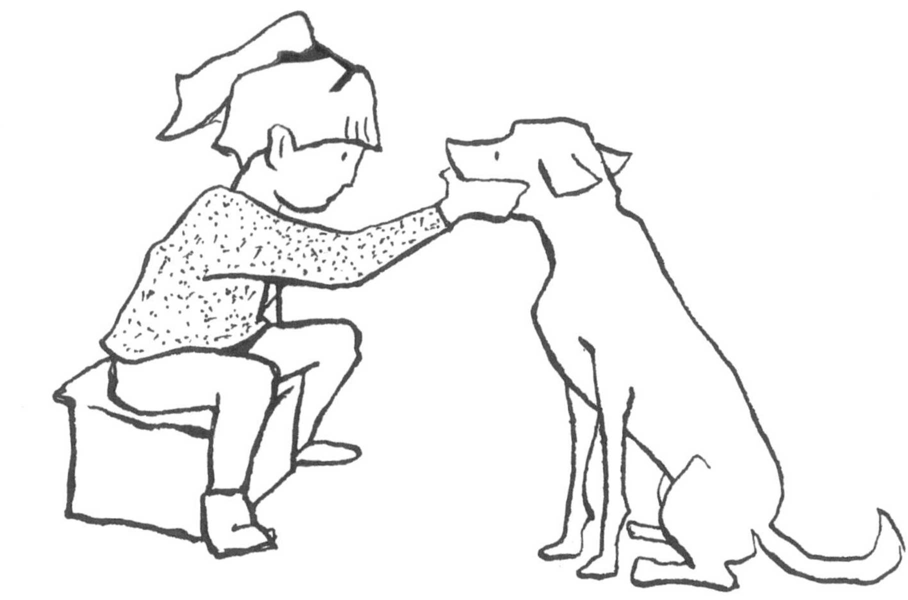

In the front room of the Grantham's house, just over from Dregs Primary, Joanna the girl had been talking to Claudia the dog all day.

'Claudie, do your talking please, show mum that trick you do where you work out about the weather.'

Mrs Grantham had begun to regret allowing Joanna to have the dog, but Joanna was an only child, and the company had seemed important.

'Oh come on Claudie,' said Joanna as she hung her arm around the dog's neck, 'show mum how you read.'

'Don't talk to Claudia like she's people, love. You're confusing her.'
Mrs Grantham had heard whispers from the neighbours that trouble lay
this way.

But Joanna couldn't stop.

She interrogated Claudia about her dog friends, about Big Socks down the
road who really did seem to love her. He was always looking and sniffing,
even when Claudia wasn't done up and hadn't fixed her hair.

'I'll help you Claud, if it comes to a wedding. I think he's a keeper,
you know? We can make you up a purple dress to go with the orange
of your skin.'

Mrs Grantham tried again to put an end to it. 'Cut it out, Joanna! That poor
thing, you'll make her think she's people.'

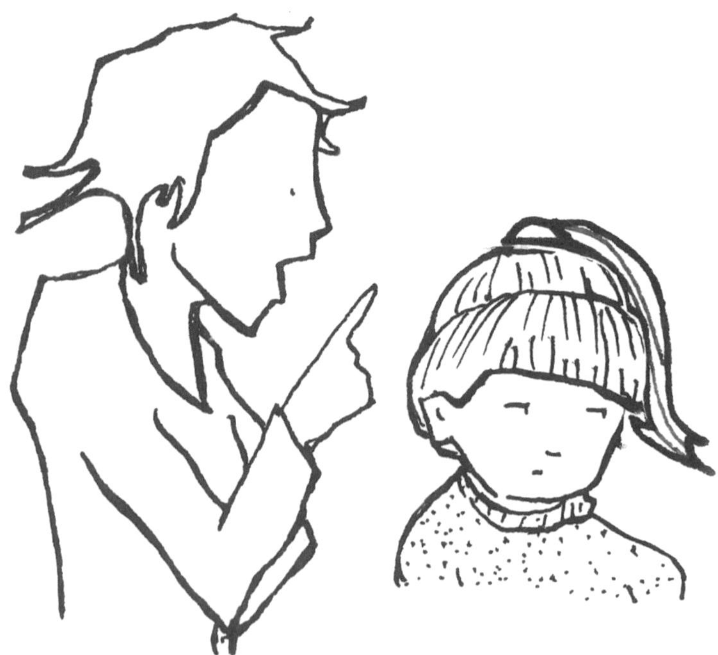

Eventually Mr Grantham came home and the talk with the dog stopped.

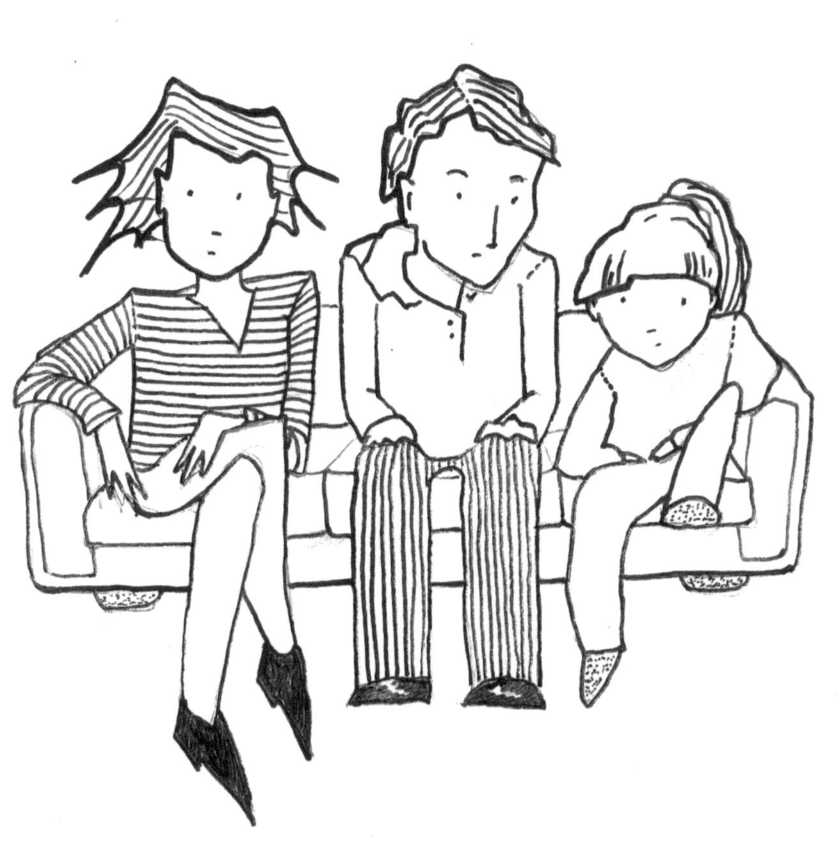

But Mr Grantham left for work each morning, every morning.
And Joanna spoke to the dog again as people. Eventually Mrs Grantham
was proven right.

People first saw proof of the trouble in February when the dog stopped
shitting in public. When Joanna walked her, Claudia snapped at other
dogs, even at the handsome ones who paid attention to her bum. At home,
Claudia abandoned the patch of attic sun for the cool guest bedroom at the
back of the house. Mrs Grantham always said cold was good for the brain.
With the attic corner unoccupied, Joanna snuck up into the sun to do her
homework but fell asleep and only woke when she heard Mrs Grantham
setting out the plates for tea.

In late March with the smell of herd pregnancies and ryegrass reaching
to the centre of town, Claudia stopped barking and gave up defending the
house from rats. Mr Grantham got a good deal on bait from Harris's but
Claudia wasn't interested even as the rats stumbled around the backyard.
Mr Grantham paid Joanna a dollar to herd the dying rats into the compost
at the back of the shed, though Mrs Grantham worried privately whether
everyone should just stick to their old jobs, lest this switch just add to
the trouble.

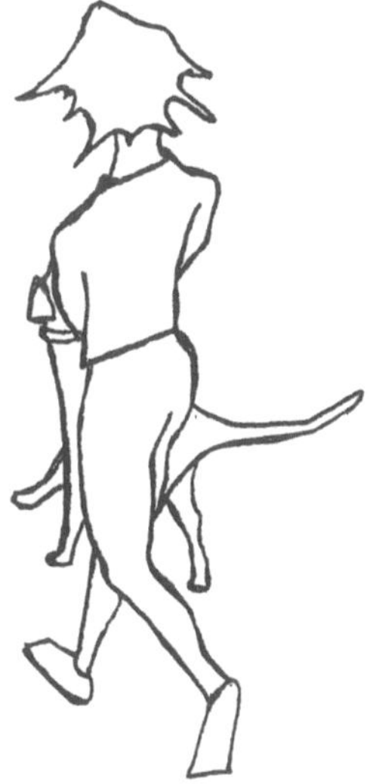

One evening that March, Joanna refused to walk Claudia on account of the dog staring at her without blinking and hissing as she approached.

'That's ridiculous Joanna, she's a dog and dogs don't hiss', her mother had said. But Joanna got the shakes and couldn't hold the leash, so Mrs Grantham walked Claudia herself. But it was evening and Joanna knew Claudia had long stopped raising her hackles at Magpie Allan over the road, so Joanna didn't know if her mother would be safe. So, after her mum and Claudia headed around the corner, Joanna crawled down the side of the house to follow in case anyone should try something on.

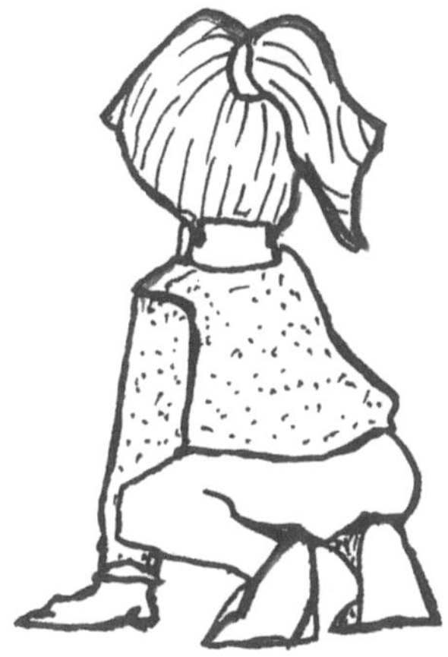

The evening was brisk and sweet-smelling and Mrs Grantham had forgiven her ratbag daughter's tantrum by the time she got to the Domain. They went on, past the rougher places on the east of town. Claudia lingered outside the flat that housed not-yet-settled young men. They were drinking out the back and called to Mrs Grantham to join them. She wasn't really thirsty, though she gave her thanks, but the dog wouldn't budge till the young men came out to pass time on the side of the street. They stroked the dog and Mrs Grantham noted she really did have to get home. But Claudia was hard to convince, turning her head as the young men said her name. The people name really had been a mistake, Mrs Grantham thought, but it was too late for that now, Claudia was what the dog answered to. Claudia finally budged when a group of girls from Dregs proper arrived and the men shifted along their attentions. Joanna crept after her mother and Claudia and wasn't noticed by anyone.

Mrs Grantham got home okay, though she felt sure daytime walks would be more seemly. Claudia outright refused to go outside with Joanna, so Mrs Grantham worked the outings into her day.

By the end of the week, Claudia began to ask for coffee. One with morning tea and one after lunch. And none of that instant stuff, please. Mrs Grantham tried to pass off Medaglio d'Oro, the very best instant in Dregs, but the dog knew, and locked her jaws around Mrs Grantham's leg until she agreed to ask Mr Mitchell at the Four Square to order in some plunger grind.

Something had gotten into the Granthams, said Mrs Mitchell when her husband told her. But they ordered it anyway.

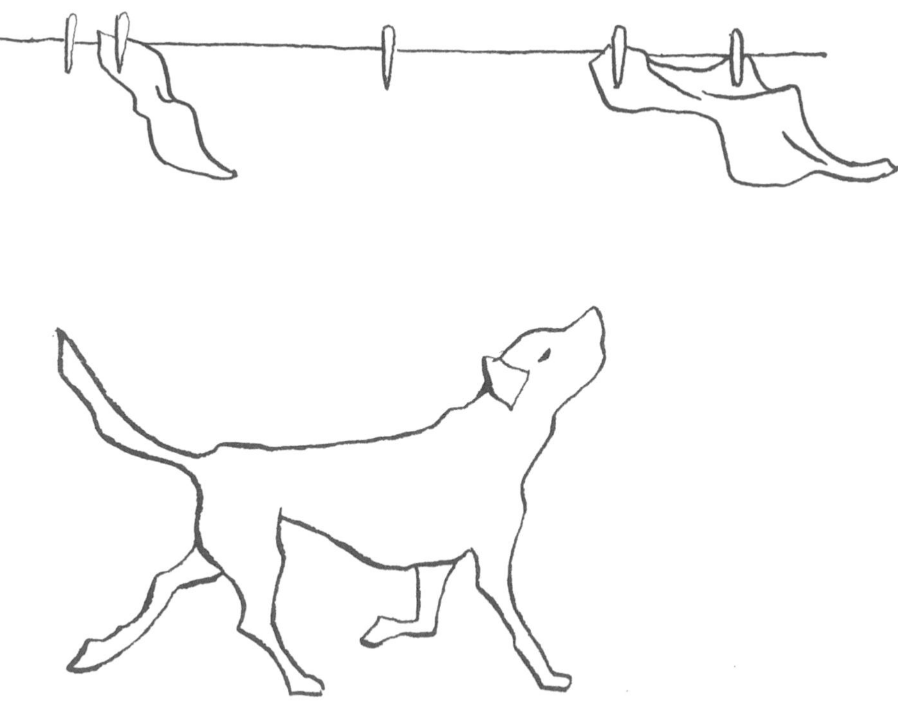

By midwinter, Claudia refused walks altogether, preferring self-directed constitutionals. She marched a line into the lawn.

'Just a refined sort of dog', a few generous townsfolk suggested.
But people had seen this course of things before. What was such a dog, bred for working life, doing in Dregs proper anyway? It was plainly asking for trouble.

Even old visiting friends from out of town swore the dog was thinking about them. And coming to conclusions. They no longer stayed long after dinner.

Since the changes, Joanna wasn't so sure about talking to Claudia to her face anymore. So she wrote her thoughts down instead:

Dear Claudia,
Please stop drinking coffee like grown ups. You're not even a citizen. Sorry you can't vote but if you tell me who you want I'll pick them for you one day. Please stop being weird. Do you know what will happen with the weather? If you do, please tell me.
From Joanna

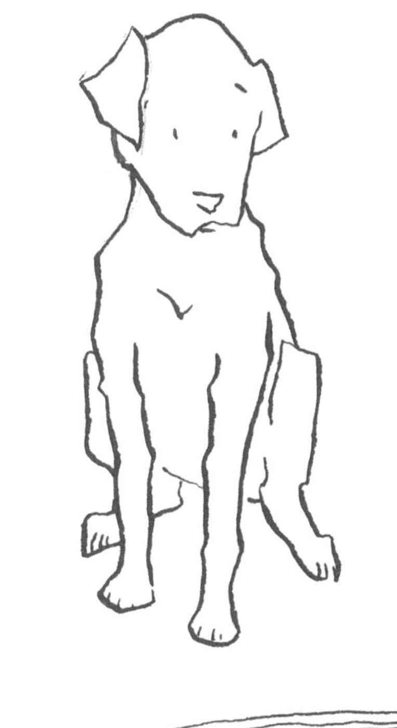

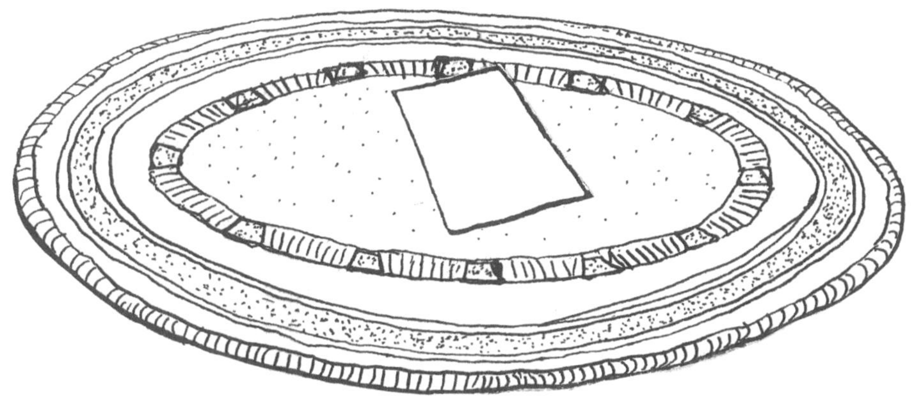

At the end of August, when the rain trapped people inside for a week,
Joanna chased mice in the warm of the attic and Claudia petitioned
Mrs Grantham to have her new status acknowledged (Joanna was asleep
again in the warm of the attic and missed the whole conversation).
Mrs Grantham had warned Joanna this trouble might happen, what with
treating Claudia like people, but she figured they'd made their bed and
in all conscience couldn't rightly refuse the dog's request. When the rain
stopped, Mrs Grantham gave Claudia directions to the JP's house and
unlocked the gate. Mrs Grantham swore on page six of the Edmonds she
would not allow Joanna any more pets.

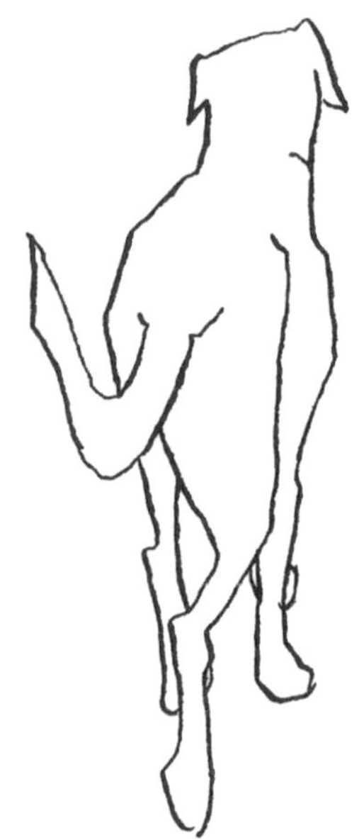

The JP was all that Claudia had hoped for. He prepared an espresso for her, which he made without asking, and which she found even nicer than coffee from the plunger, and he stroked her soft coat as he wrote up her citizenship application. He played with the loose furry skin on her back. It was an unusual case, he acknowledged, but he was skilled, and had done this for years, so she'd come to just the right place. He might have to make a few phone calls to secure it, but should it work out, her certificate would be in the mail.

Claudia stepped out the door. The JP leant against the frame: 'What I wouldn't give to have a young thing like you to warm my bed.' Claudia chuckled uncomfortably, politely, as she turned towards the gate. She wondered if this indulgence might hurry things along. That seemed fair. So she dealt the JP three minutes with the secrets under her fur in exchange for the citizenship papers to take home. Today.

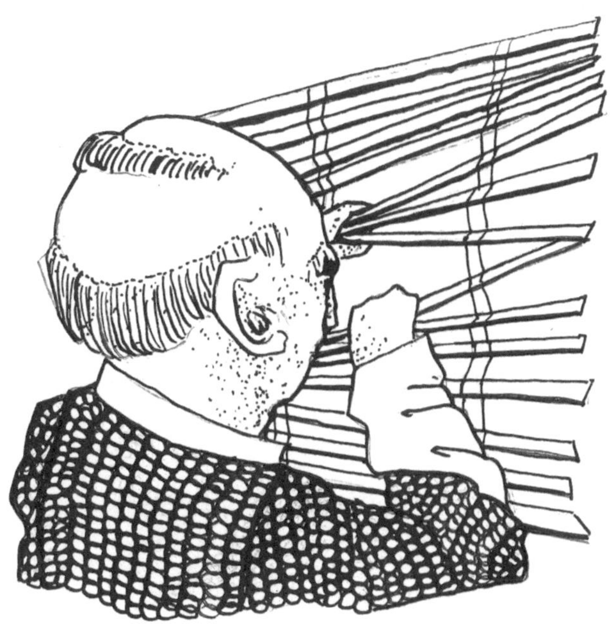

And Claudia took the papers home.

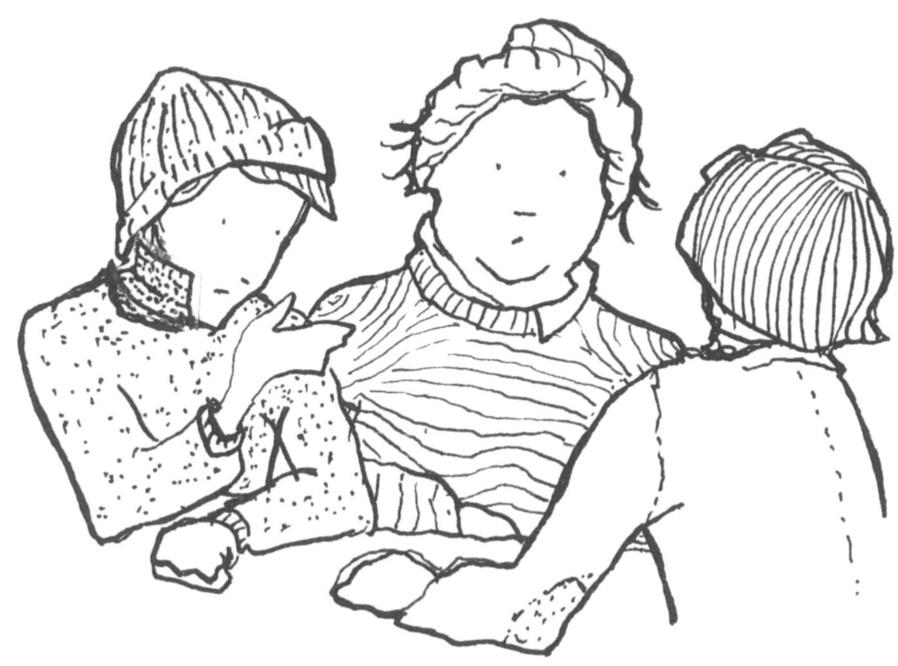

All over the countryside, people knew something was up. Gaylene Metcalfe said the Umbridge's ewes had all cast themselves, and not one of them pregnant or long ago shorn. Mrs McKercher-Briggs had been cooking for the shearers down at their family flock in Temoana. Her sheep weren't so temperamental as the Umbridge's, and were all right side up, but not a shearer had got through his lunch. 'They're sensitive ones, that crew; they smell when something's gone odd, even before the livestock. And what's more, Tall Frederick's eels didn't come to him today, though he hadn't fed them yesterday and they should have been crazy for meat.'

Soon the wind was up all of Dregs. The Nicholsons got funny about their cats and locked them in crates as if they'd been raised for farm work and Mrs Holdaway's mushrooms grew orange and tasted of sweat. Peyton McGrath returned all the letters he'd never delivered so that little reunions and brand-new feuds broke out all over town. Mrs O'Donnell finally worked it out when the bitches came on heat and her Big Socks didn't even look at Claudia. In the past, it had always taken at least two people to hold him back. 'She's pregnant.'

Mrs Grantham shuddered. Claudia was not a wandering bitch. It could only have been that once. And that meant not a puppy, but a thing. She worried what the Arts and Plants Committee would think.

Claudia sat out back with her plunger. She was now having at least 11 cups a day. Surely the thing inside her would be damaged enough already. But Dregs was lucky, it would all be contained. Mrs Grantham ran a clean home and, being a child of this, Claudia understood. She called the vet herself and asked that she fix up the trouble.

And cats again stalked the night, for better or worse, and mushrooms tasted like mushrooms. Peyton was moved to the sorting room out back under the careful eye of new cameras lest his incomplete delivery habits, long suspected now known, should return. Martha Chisholm, in the back room for almost two decades, was pleased for the chance to be out on the round, and smiled each day at the sun.

At the vet's they flushed the thing, good riddance, unclean and unholy. Claudia's friends took her for coffee at the milk bar in the middle of town. They were tea drinkers usually, but curious.

Joanna, now quite skilled in her trailing, had watched the thing as it flushed. She called it back home through the plumbing. At night, at the back of the house, she dropped food through the outside grating.
And in the day she played there by herself.

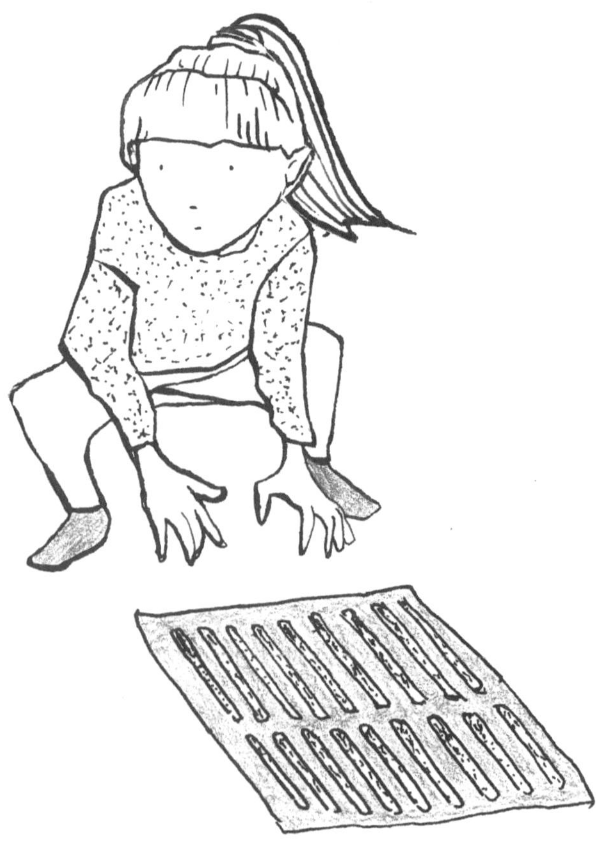

Fear and trembling in the Little Uplands: The Giant Himalayan Lily to spawn at last

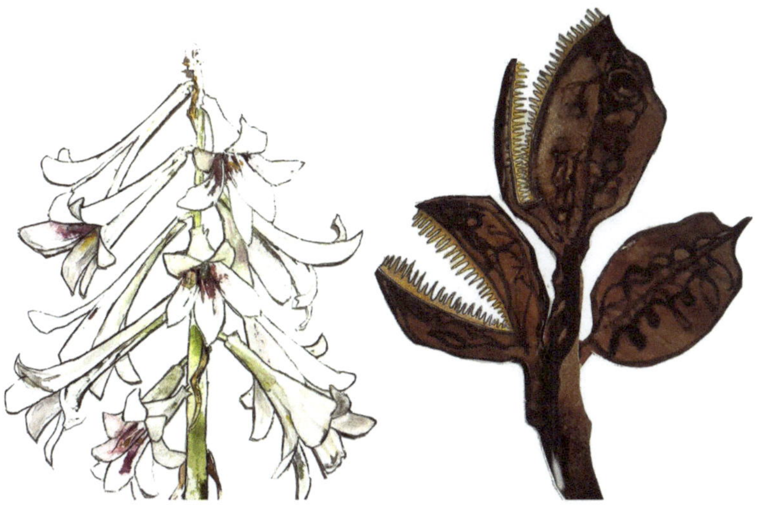

The flowers (left) and ornamental pods (right) of *Cardiocrinum giganteum*, the Giant Himalayan Lily that will soon emerge in the Little Uplands en masse, the product of a likely seed bombing almost seven years ago.

Lilies of a number of varieties have a curious history in Dregs and surrounds, with cases of mass uprisings of these usually exclusive flowers becoming something of a trend in the region over the past decade. It has only been in the last several years, however, that locals have become accustomed to large numbers of *Cardiocrinum giganteum*, the Giant Himalayan Lily, and, as we enter a new phase in the plant's life cycle, residents of the Little Uplands are particularly anxious to know how it will integrate into our town.

As no record of the human introduction of *Cardiocrinum giganteum* plants in the area has been found, the leading theory is that they first arrived in the fur of Himalayan Tahr. Whatever the story of their initial arrival, lilies can now be found throughout Dregs proper and surrounds. They have particularly flourished in the Little Uplands, where they can be found towering on average 2 metres high on green verges across the suburb. The large numbers of plants in the area have raised suspicions of a deliberate seed bombing some years ago.

A late bloomer, taking up to seven years to flower, the development of flower buds has been noted by residents of the suburb, who have expressed both excitement and trepidation about future developments. While a number of residents are set to welcome the blooms, hosting viewing parties across the suburb, some have expressed caution about the looming arrival of the plant's seed pods, both on account of their fearsome appearance and abundant fertility.

Dying after it flowers, the *Cardiocrinum giganteum* releases thousands of seeds before retiring into ornamental pods, as will soon be visible throughout the region to unknown effect.

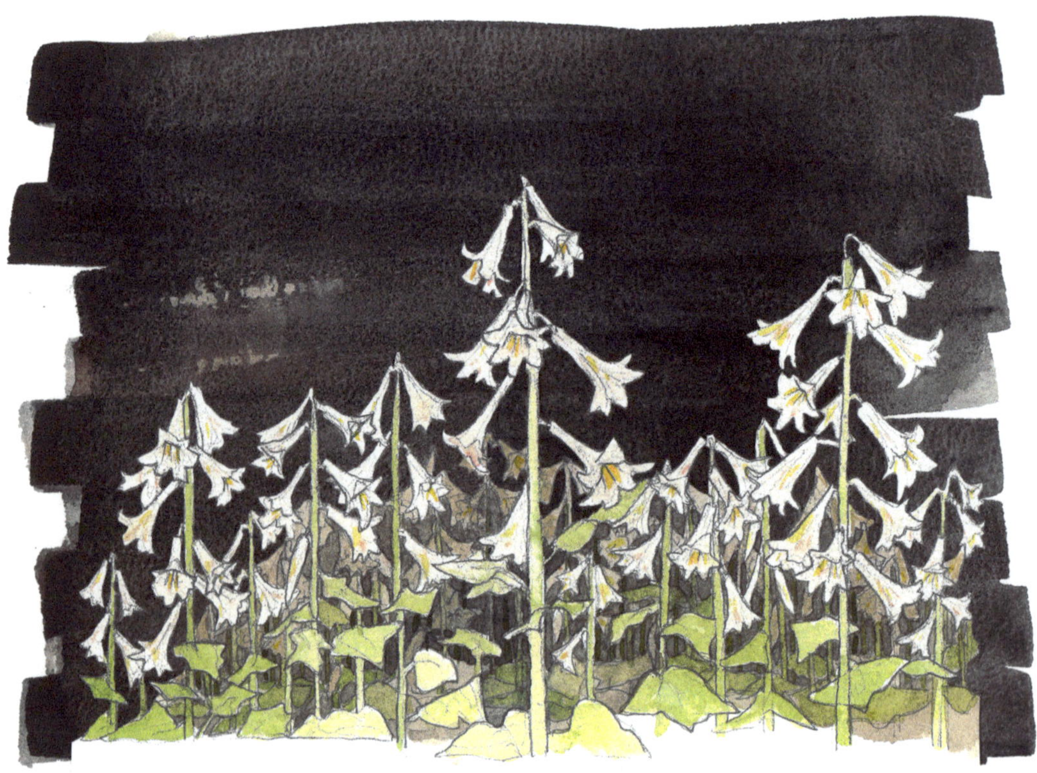

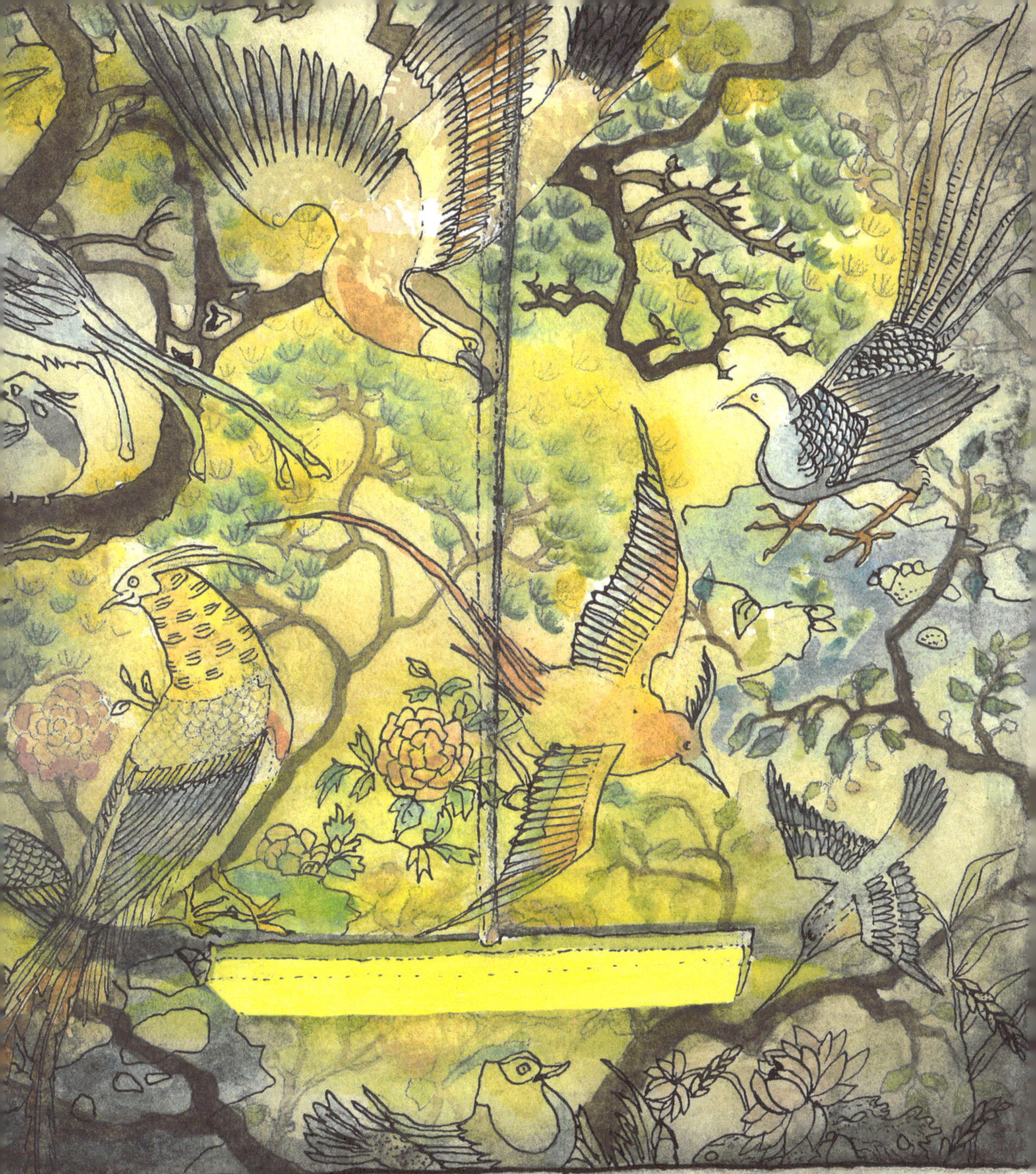

SH £ CHIPS   HAMBURGER   OTHER

FISH & CHIPS		HAMBURGER		OTHER	
(BATTERED)	$2.00	PLAIN BURGER	$3.50	ONION RINGS (DOZ)	$3.00
(CRUMBED)	$2.50	CHEESE BURGER	$4.00	HASH BROWNS	$1.00
(S (SCOOP)	$2.00	EGG BURGER	$4.00	CHICKEN NUGGETS	50c
ARA CHIPS	$3.30	HAWAIIAN BURGER	$4.50	PINEAPPLE RINGS (2)	$1.00
Y WEDGES	$3.00	STEAK BURGER	$5.00	SQUID RINGS	$1.00
DOGS	$1.80	BACON BURGER	$4.50	½ DOZ OYSTERS (BLUFF)	$10.00
SAGE	$1.50	CHICKEN BURGER	$4.50	1 DOZ OYSTERS "	$16.00
NG ROLL	$2.00	FISH BURGER	$4.50	½ DOZ SCALLOPS	$8.00
RY ROLL	$2.00	EXTRAS: BEETROOT, TOMATO 50c		½ DOZ MUSSELS	$5.00
B STICKS	$1.50	EGG, CHEESE, PINEAPPLE $1.00		SCALLOP (POTATO)	$1.00

MB/BATTER	CRUMB/BATTER	CRUMB/BATTER	WONTONS	DIM SIMS	PRAWN CRACKERS
BLUE COD	SOLE FILLET	TERAKIHI	60c EACH	50c EACH	
$5.00	$4.30	$4.50	$5.00/DOZEN	$4.00/DOZEN	$2.00/BAG

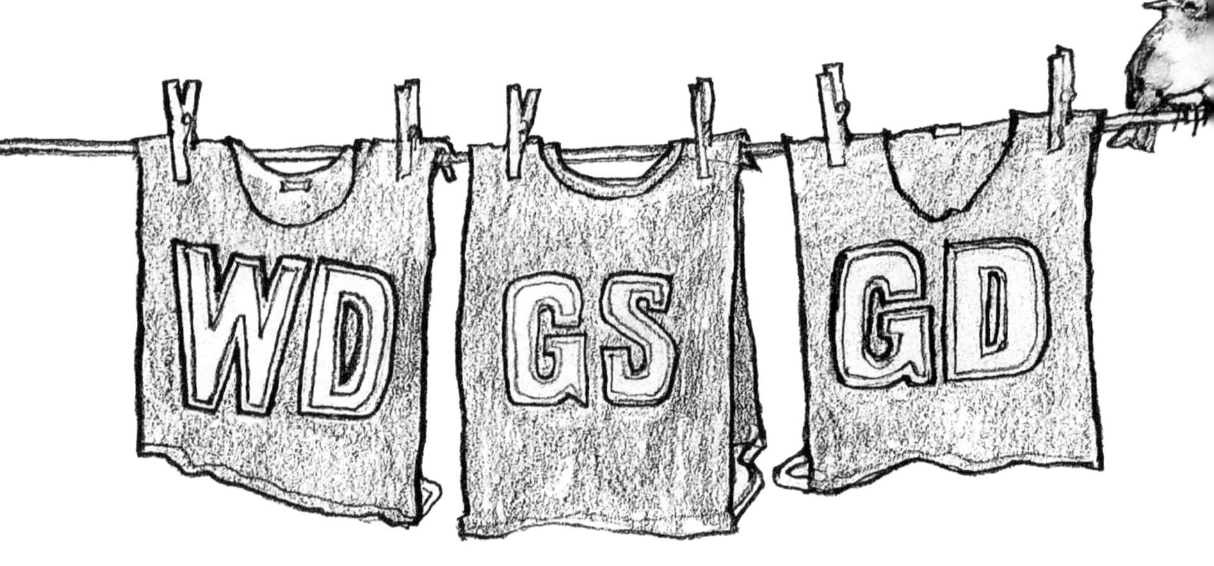

WD
GS
GD

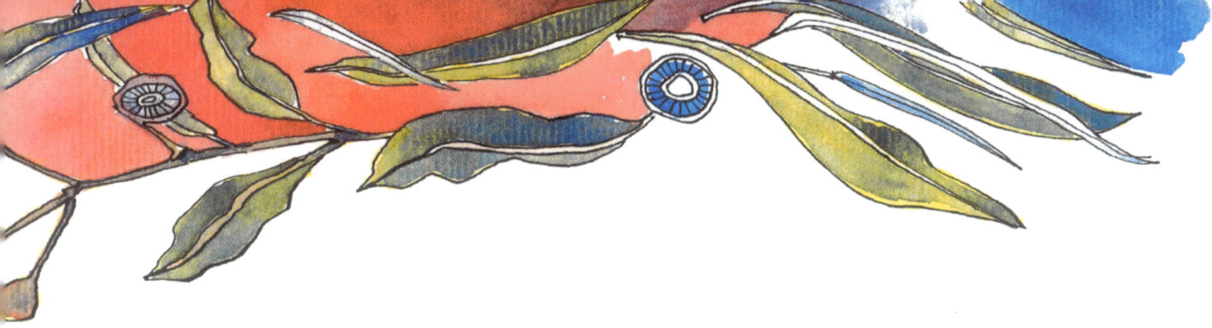

A quiet story

Christopher Martin's story is small and quiet. It is also one that hasn't ended. He was and is no sweeter than other folks in Dregs, but he realised soon enough that his tenderness wasn't something that could just be turned off. Behind the cottage he shared with his mum was a patch of eucalypt trees born the same week as him and that his mother hadn't had the heart to cut down. And on the days that it was too much, all that feeling without any rest, he took everything back there to them, the trees seeming able and willing to hold things, even though they were all the same age.

At 10, the trees had mostly reached their full heights, but Christopher would grow a few years taller still. He inspired some quiet chatter the winter before he turned 13, when he had played goal shoot for Tauhou, which his mum said also meant stranger, but also that cute little bird that loves all the nectar. There had been no rule written against it, with no-one having imagined a boy even wanting to play netball. On competition days, he wore his winter school shorts, shorts the very same grey as Tauhou's uniform skirts, and folks commented on the odd sense of ease of it all. That season they'd won, something the club wasn't well known for, unruly as their teams tended to be. Several girls retired from the sport after that win, figuring they had had the best, so why not try something else. And, in time, girls from that team became famous for martial arts, whitewater rafting and competitive avant-garde hairdressing, which are stories that are also ongoing.

A group stayed friends after the team was disbanded and later, when Alice the ex-wing defence got her driver's licence (she was always going to be the first of the bunch), they started a habit of heading up to Christopher's for tea on a Wednesday.

And Christopher lived through the years of the cloud though, like anyone, not without heartache. Each time the clouds had rolled in, Christopher felt it in his cells, which would vibrate so fast it seemed he might rip right apart at any moment. But near the eucalypts it would stop and he'd find himself once again breathing out. So, in those times, he'd stayed close to the grove and, on harder nights, slept leaning against the smooth wood of one tree or another, until his mum returned in the small hours after her shift, and led him gently back to his bed.

Though he didn't tend to ask things in class, and the cloud itself was never discussed, one day at school in a discussion on health, he'd asked whether others also found comfort with trees and, if so, with which particular kinds. Kids had laughed, Mrs Crenshaw too, but Ruthie, who still played goal defence for the old team and treasured Christopher for each win, even though he was now two seasons retired, glared at each and every person in the room with a stare that looked like death and Alice stood beside her and all the laughing stopped. But no-one answered the question, not even Alice or Ruthie who had so wanted to say they found such comfort too, and with which kinds of trees, so that Christopher wouldn't be so all alone. But, back then, they didn't know what he meant about the trees, so they hadn't been able to say. Christopher stayed quiet through it all and the eucalypts, even back up at home as they were, pulled him close.

On the week of the fires, Christopher found he could stand the flames and he managed to hose in water enough to dowse the blazes next door and down at numbers 87, 89 and 91 where the flames had leapt straight in from the Edgelands. The homes made it through the week whole, apart from their burnt gutter edges. The netball girls had wondered how it was that he wasn't even a little singed and they'd teased him for being something like fireproof. But he'd smiled only slightly, so they'd dropped it.

The volunteer fire crew in Dregs back then was mostly men with farms not too far from the township or with their own contracting gigs and who thus had no bosses to be troubled by the interruptions. They'd heard of Christopher, though no-one recalled having ever really met him, him having never played rugby. Josh Grover, finding himself in charge of new recruits in his menteeship for the fire committee chair, checked in with Rewi Clarke at the rugby club after his Saturday golden oldie match to see if he might have known Christopher through something cultural. But the boy, Rewi said, wasn't from anywhere around here and he knew nothing more than did Josh. But Dregs is a small town after all, so when Christopher finished school and Josh heard he'd found a job in the council buildings in town, he popped around for a chat to see if he might join the volunteers, and he would. And Christopher would prove himself a fine recruit with a knack for the flames and Josh found himself with many pats on the back, as kids like Christopher didn't tend to join. But Christopher would never join for an after-call-out drink, even when the men felt he'd really earned a shout. He never said no directly to the offers, but was just gone before anyone knew.

Just after Christopher's mother got sick a man, also young, but from Timaru, came to visit and stayed through the months she was ill, and stayed on even after she'd passed. He drove back to Timaru daily for work. Through the years Christopher kept that same job in Dregs, in charge of the full council archives. He ran that archival office by himself with a calm that made the quick turnaround a consistently sweet little shock. When the fire bells rang he would put his current file back in the box of to-dos and, quiet as you like, check the classified cabinet was well-locked, and then place the sign in the window explaining he'd be back as soon as circumstances allowed.

The girls still visited on Wednesdays, and other than them and his gentleman, Christopher tended to not see so many people. But he knew the trees, and felt they somehow knew him even more. Sometimes someone new to town would ask about Christopher, about why he had that shimmering scent of lemon and wood something quite green, and would wonder if there was something about him perhaps a bit strange. But the netball girls would wave the question away with a hand, noting that that was just Christopher and he somehow just smells good.

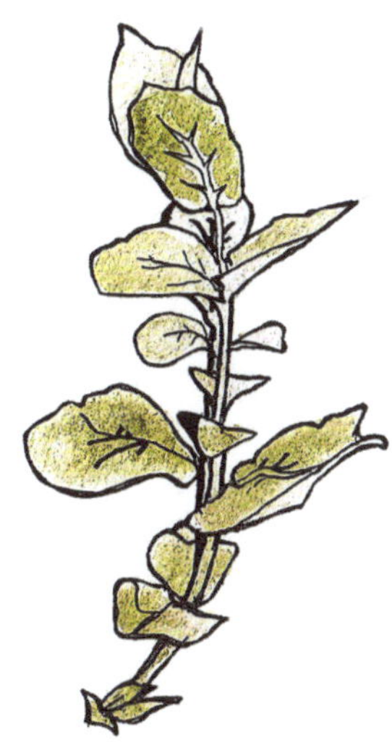

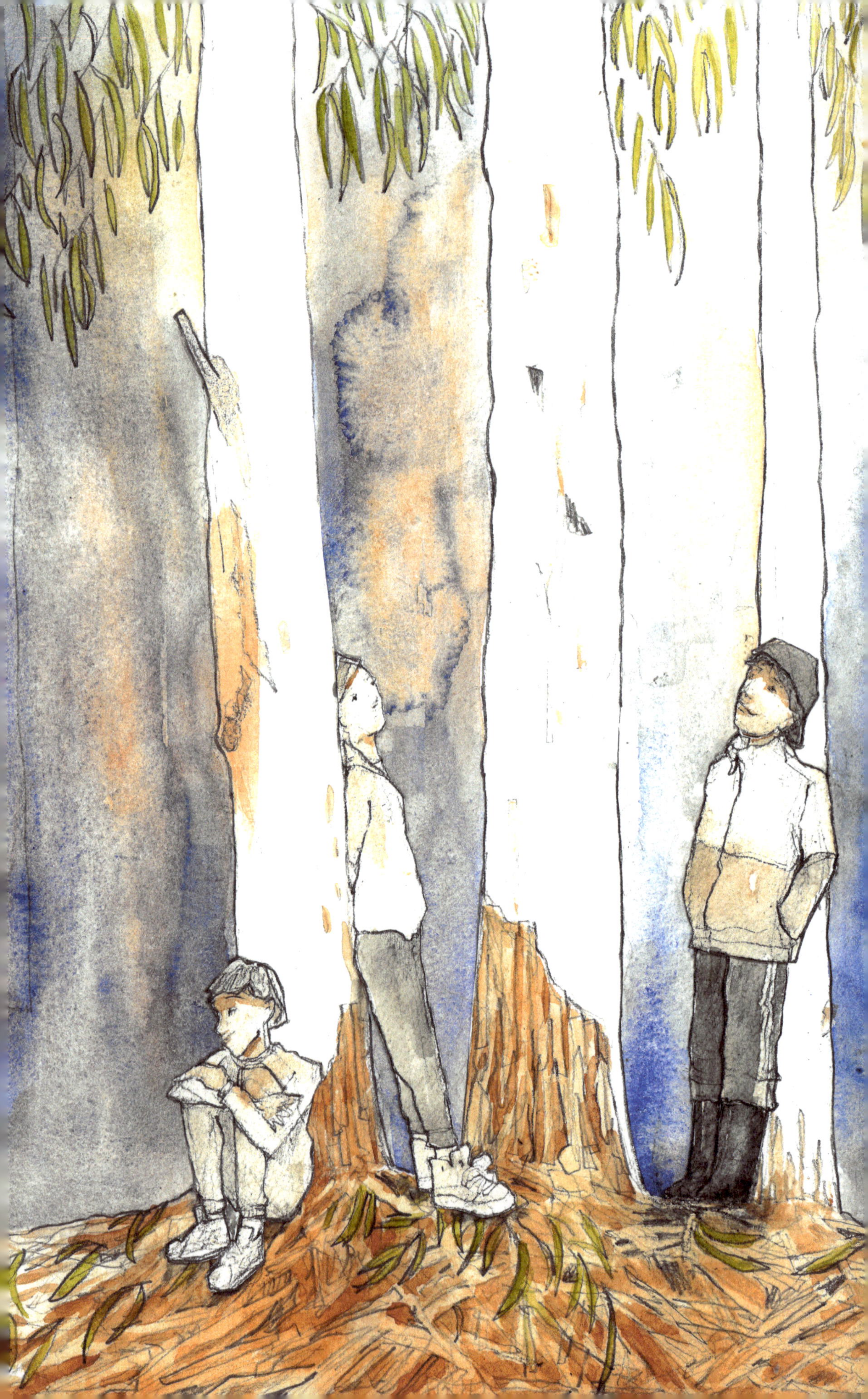

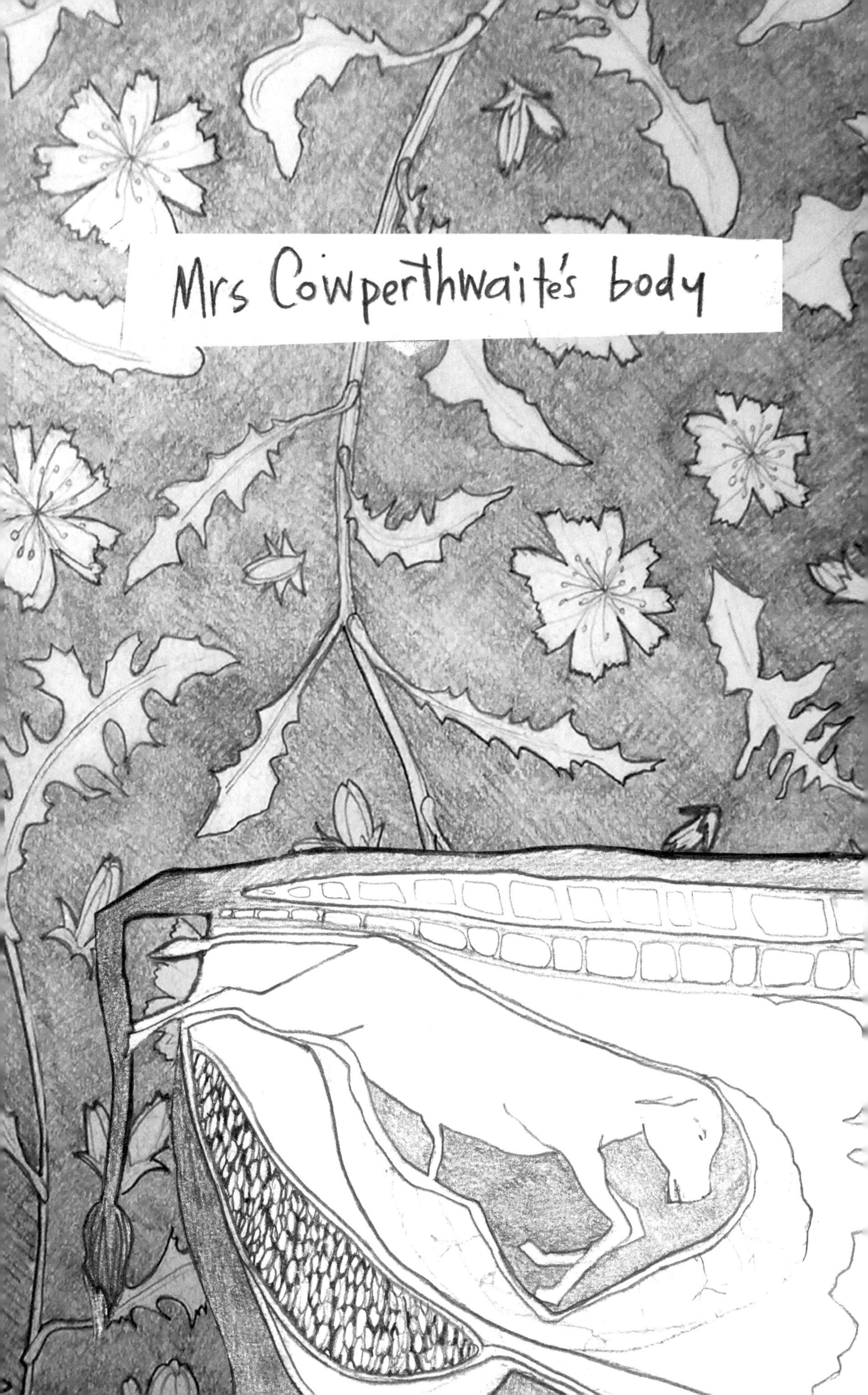

Mrs Cowperthwaite's body

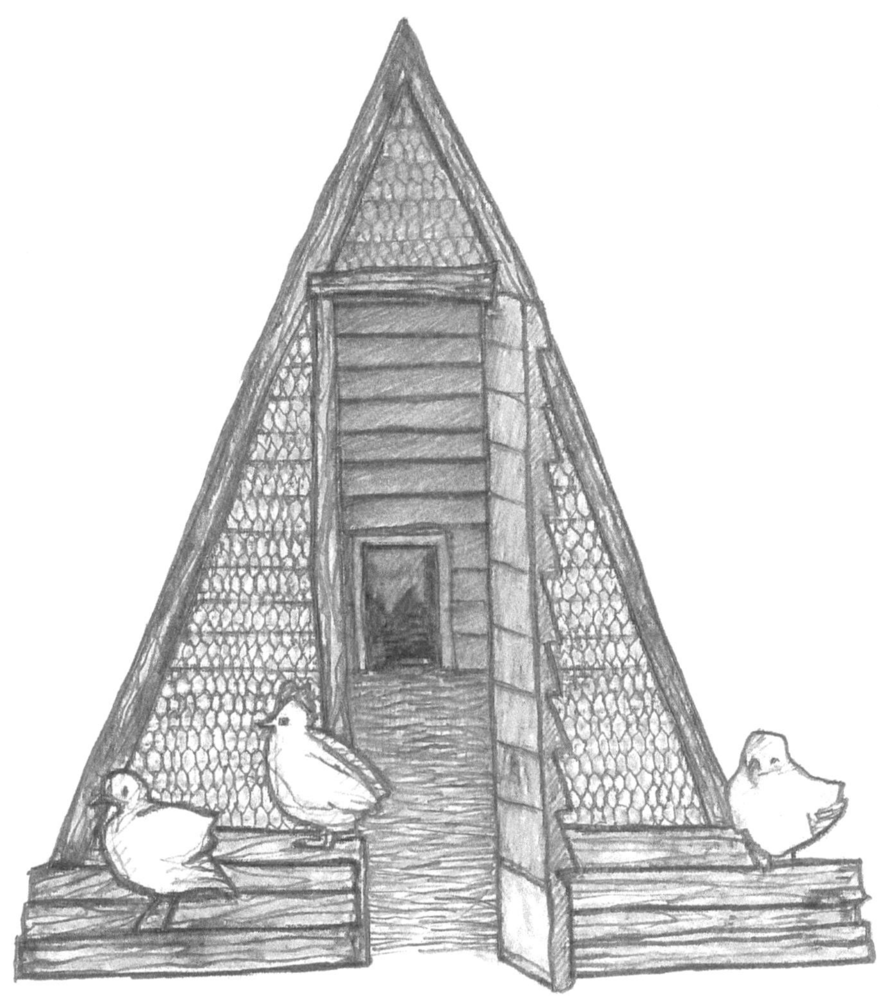

Tom Cowperthwaite was the only boy of his dad, so the farm was always going to be his. It was a large sheep station in the back of the Western Dip where Tom's sister and a girl called Sally had taught their Barbies to fuck. In the Cowperthwaite chicken hutch where the girls always played, the Barbies cut off their hair to the meanest of bobs and each forced her pointy hand at the other to try to forge a cunt, taking breaks to cook and to vacuum until it got too dark to see.

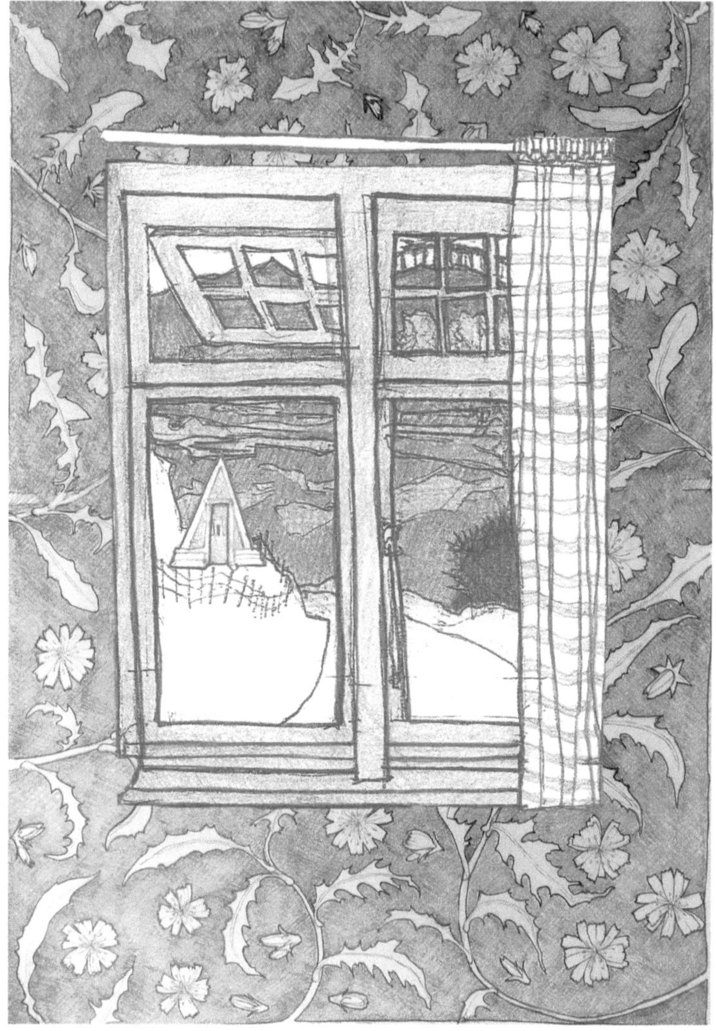

Tom and Sally married in not too long, though Sally wasn't from the high country, so no-one was sure how it would turn out. But Tom didn't mind. In a short while, Tom and the new Mrs Cowperthwaite had an heir and two girls (nice for their mother) all three years apart.

At those three babies, Mrs Cowperthwaite figured she'd done her duty, so, after the youngest left for boarding school, she sailed to Perth with Tom's sister who needed to make a living. They listened to Emmylou Harris as they travelled and Mrs Cowperthwaite thought that Tom's sister's profile, which was almost straight from her forehead to her nose, had a look of Persian royalty. They never came back. Mrs Cowperthwaite left her body here with Tom on account of their promising God that their bodies would stay always paired. She left him a note to care for it.

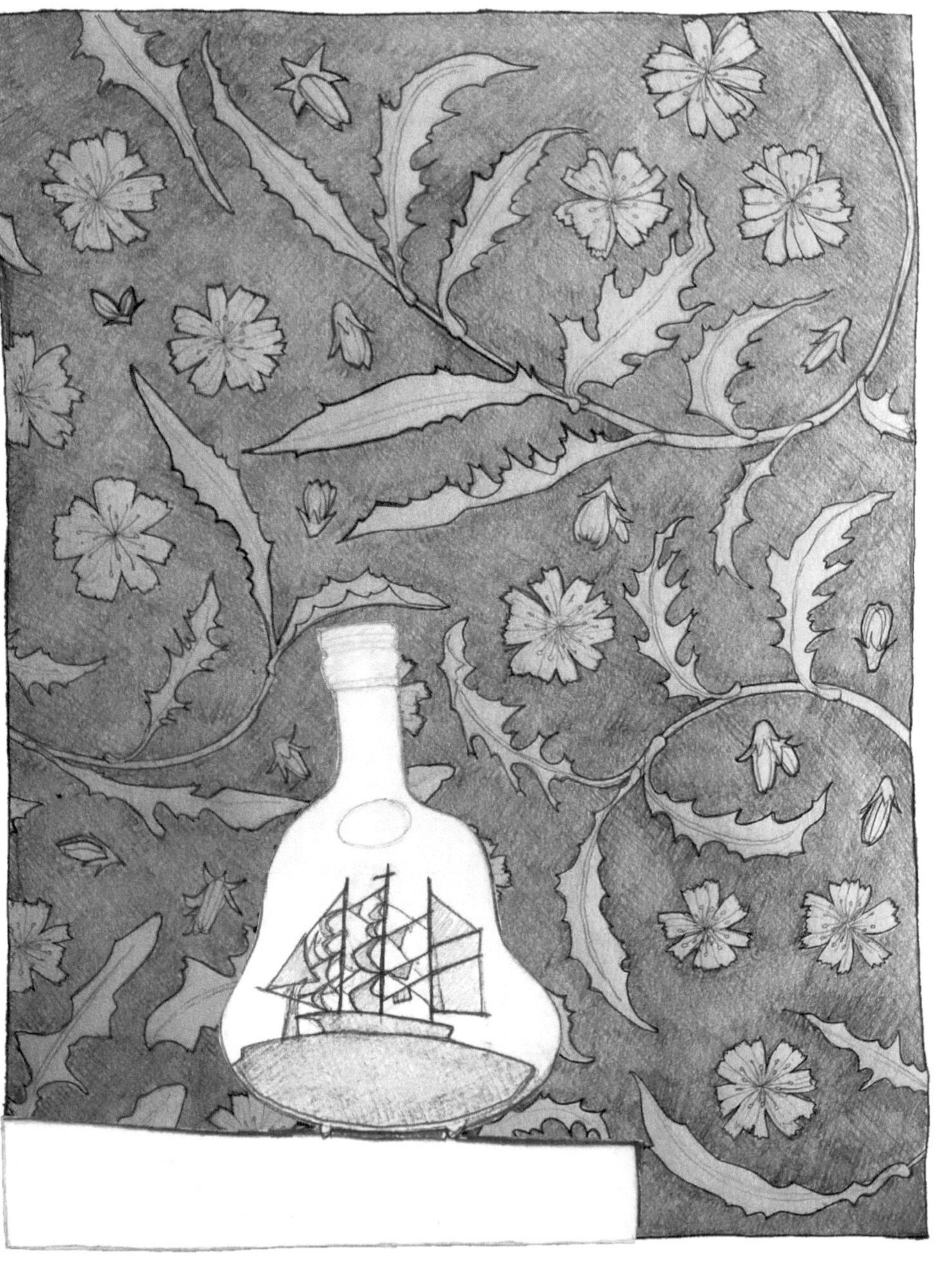

And Tom did care for it. He showered the body and dried it, fed and warmed it and touched it in ways he hadn't when Mrs Cowperthwaite was still here. He spoke to the body quietly and gently and asked his mother to come over one day a week to wash and press the body's Aertex shirts and its Moleskins. Seven days of fresh underwear and two cotton bras were washed in sensitive liquid and the body's variously patterned socks were fluffy and bundled into perfect balls. Tom's mother placed the clothes, neatly folded (except for the shirts, which were hung), back in the drawers. After his mother left, Tom placed sprigs of lavender in among them.

He began new shopping lists of everything he could think that the body might need. There was to be A2 cream and alfredo sauce and strawberries, salami and cheeses. Sweet cool yoghurt and Earl Grey tea. The farm was in fine condition and finances were also fine. He worked the near paddock and planted barley and comfrey and asparagus. He called his boy back from school to help with the animals in which he found he was no longer so interested.

On the body's birthday, Tom arranged for his mother to take his son and in the night he turned the concert station on low and threw scarves over the lights. He undressed the body tenderly and covered it with oil and warmed it and fixed its hair and slipped himself inside.

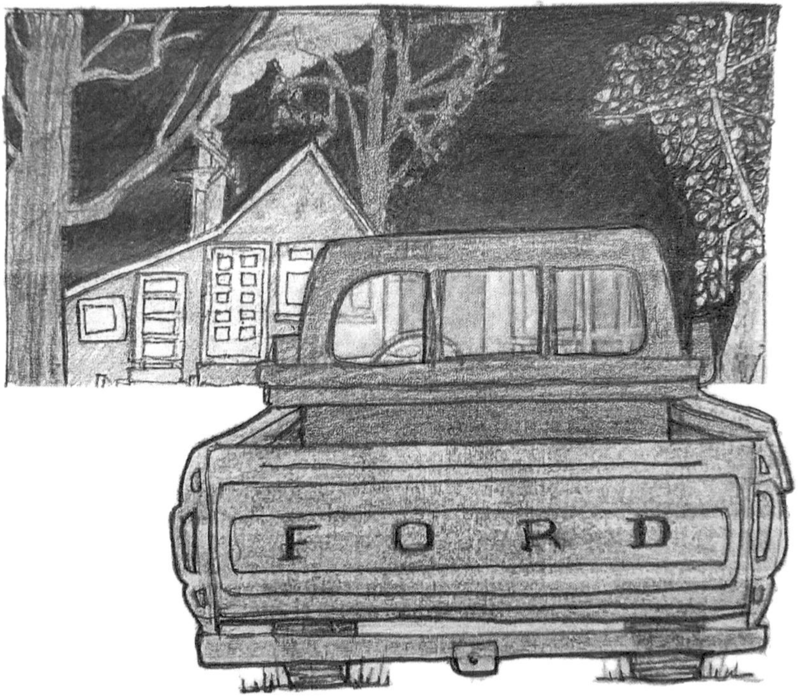

It wasn't long until the body was pregnant. He'd taken the body a fortnight before it was due to the Women's Hospital in Timaru, paying privately just in case extra help had been needed. But it hadn't been needed; the birth easy and remarkably sweet. Mr Cowperthwaite loved the baby. He would smell it and hold it, and he asked his son to take over the running of the farm completely so that he could love the baby and the body full-time. Tom moved with the body into the back cottage and his son stayed in the main house. Another baby came, then more. In the night he turned on the porch lights of the back cottage and started up the radio in the ute and held the body and all the new children and they danced and they danced. Blossoms then leaves then snow in turn and he held the body and the children warm and they danced.

The body died after the fifth child, having already been along in years when they began. Local people held Mr Cowperthwaite back as they lowered the casket, and, back at the farm, passed him from person to person all that night (with three at all times to hold him). He let out moans that made people shy, but they held on to him anyway. When his watchers finally fell asleep, he ran, down through the valley to the field out the back of St Martha's where the body was buried. He dug and dug through the shit and the soil, tore at the casket and cracked it open with a stone. He reunited with the body to which he called out things that no-one around here had ever heard before, only read, so we didn't know they sounded that way, and he vowed to the body that he wouldn't leave it and he pushed himself hard up inside it and wouldn't leave, even when we warned him that the body needed to be covered up again by earth, and that if he didn't get up, get out of there, we'd have no choice but to cover him, too. But he held on to the body as if he hadn't heard, and we'd all heard his promise to it, so we had no choice but to cover them up together.

Tom loved that body. Everyone had to agree.

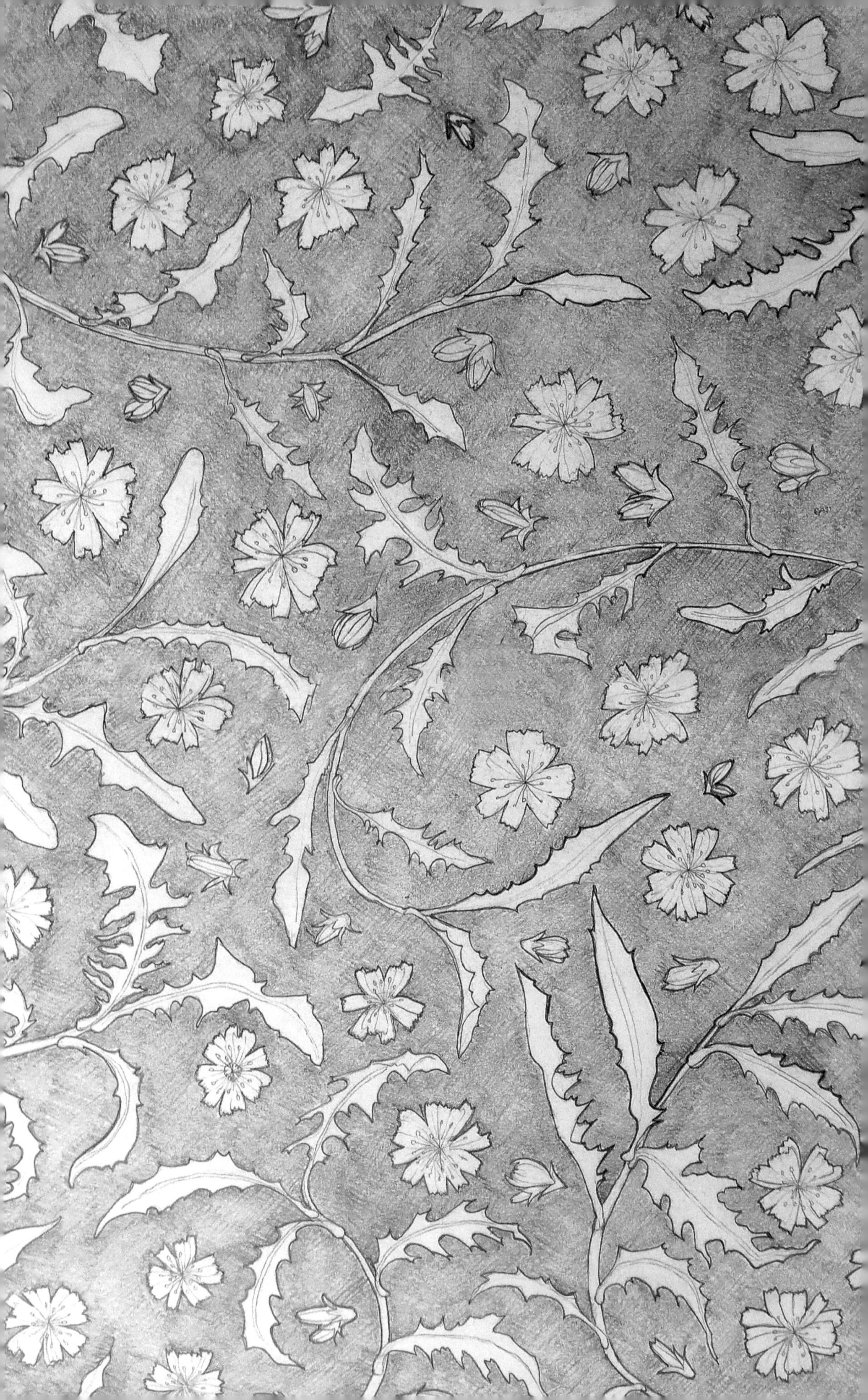

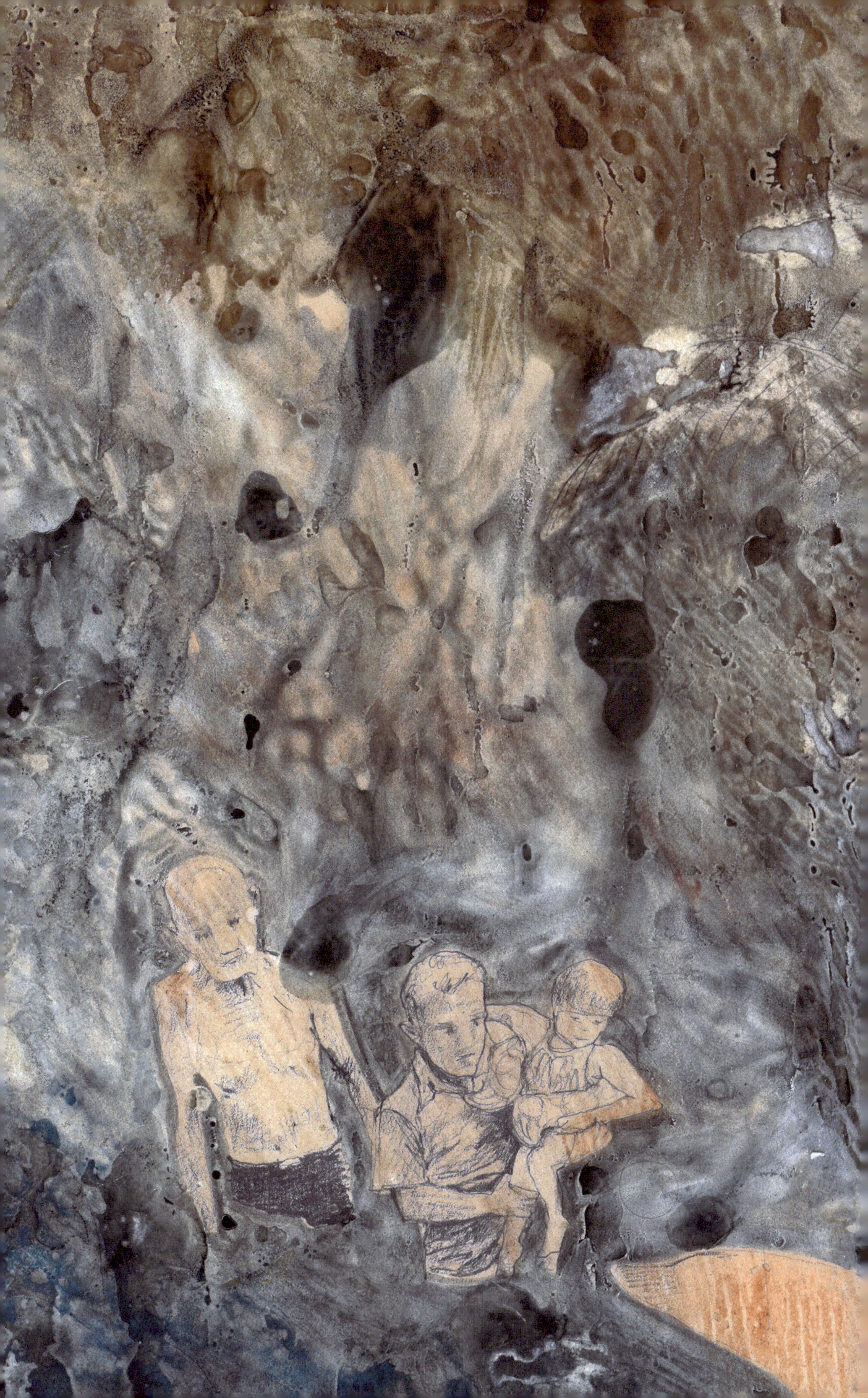

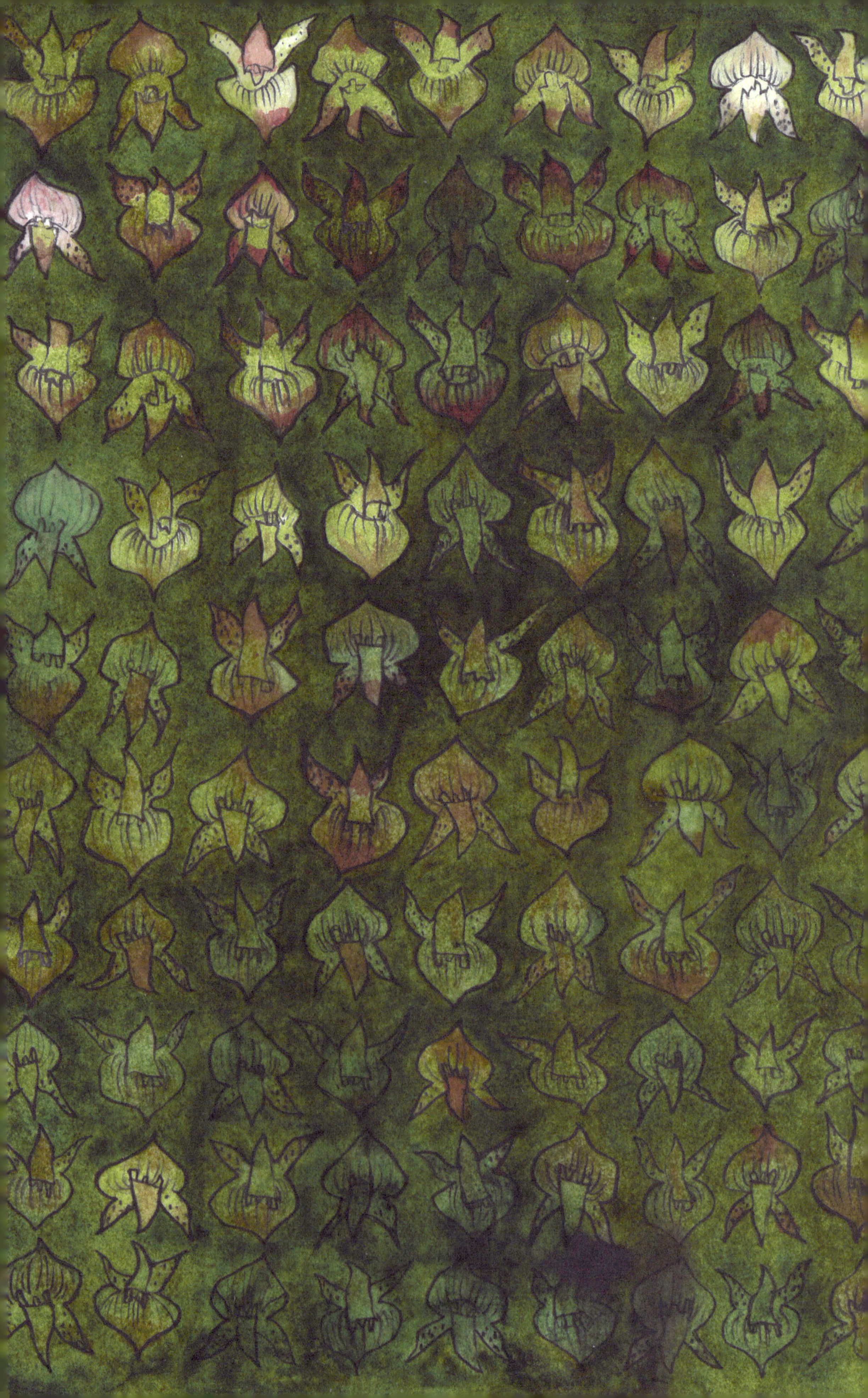

Glossary

This list is a preliminary glossary based on questions raised by readers. Further queries are welcomed by the author, and readers are welcome to submit their own suggestions.

A2 milk

A2 milk is a form of cow's milk that carries little of a variety of β-casein proteins called A1. While arguments about the health benefits of such milk continue, in the late 1990s and early 2000s when these stories were set, the preference for A2 milk (from cow breeds such as Jersey and Guernsey) was not in line with mainstream milk production in Aotearoa/New Zealand, due to both legal clashes with Fonterra, New Zealand's largest milk company, and, relatedly, because the majority of New Zealand's cows produce A1 milk.

Bracelets (permanent)

Although at the time of publication, permanent jewellery was becoming a hit among the Kardashians, it was, in rural 1990s South Canterbury, already a thing among some of the wealthier rural families, in which bracelets would be put on babies or young girls and added to as they grow.

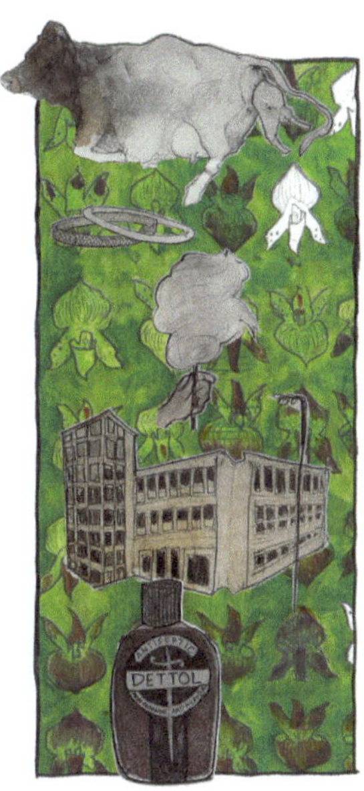

Candy floss

Is a confection common at fairs made of spun sugar with a cotton-like appearance. Also known as cotton candy (US) or fairy floss (Australia).

Cherry Farm

A psychiatric hospital near Dunedin, Cherry Farm opened in 1952 and closed in 1992. Although its use of a village-asylum model was in stark contrast to previous more fortress-type models of psychiatric hospitals (such as Seacliff Lunatic Asylum just north of Dunedin or Sunnyside Mental Hospital in Christchurch), it remained something of a threat in the face of misbehaviour.

Dettol

Originally formulated in the United Kingdom, Dettol was introduced to New Zealand in 1935. Using chloroxylenol as its active ingredient, it is still widely used as an antiseptic and disinfectant.

Edmonds cookbook

Famous in New Zealand for its relatively simple recipes for traditional New Zealand fare, such as scones, roasts and pikelets, the Edmonds Cookery Book was originally a marketing booklet; first published in 1908, it was sent free to housewives who requested it. While it is no longer free, it remains popular throughout the country, having sold over 3 million copies.

Guy Fawkes

A commemoration of the thwarted plot of Guy Fawkes to blow up the House of Lords as part of the 'Gunpowder Plot' of 1605, Guy Fawkes Night, on 5 November, is a popular celebration throughout New Zealand where it takes on much of the tone of Northern Hemisphere Beltane/early summer celebrations. Its history, although often overlooked, is rooted in pro-Protestant, anti-Catholic sentiment, as Fawkes was a committed Catholic and the burning of an effigy or 'Guy' was historically the central event of Guy Fawkes commemoration. The burning of the Guy is becoming less common and, increasingly, the night is known as 'Fireworks Night', taking on more of a Beltane mood.

Hooker

See Scrum, rugby

JP

In New Zealand, a JP, or justice of the peace is a person of good reputation nominated by a local member of parliament and appointed by the governor-general to sign and witness a range of legal documents. In New Zealand, JPs are not paid.

Lions

Lions Clubs are part of an international service network. Along with Rotary Clubs, Lions Clubs play an important community role in many South Canterbury towns, with many activities and fundraisers being organised by such groups. Such groups are also important for socialising and networking within and between towns.

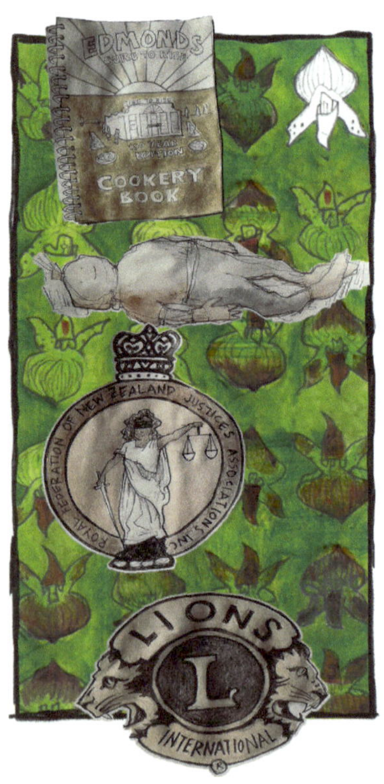

Lock

See Scrum, rugby

Loosehead prop

See Scrum, rugby

Scrum, rugby

In rugby union, a scrum is a method of restarting play in which players (the forwards) pack closely together in an attempt to gain possession of the ball, which is fed into the scrum by one team's half-back (or scrum-half as they are known in other countries). Please see diagram below for positions. Using New Zealand parlance, the numbers signal the following positions: 1: loosehead prop; 2: hooker; 3: tighthead prop; 4: lock; 5: lock; 6: blindside flanker; 7: openside flanker; 8: number 8; 9: half-back.

Tighthead prop

See Scrum, rugby

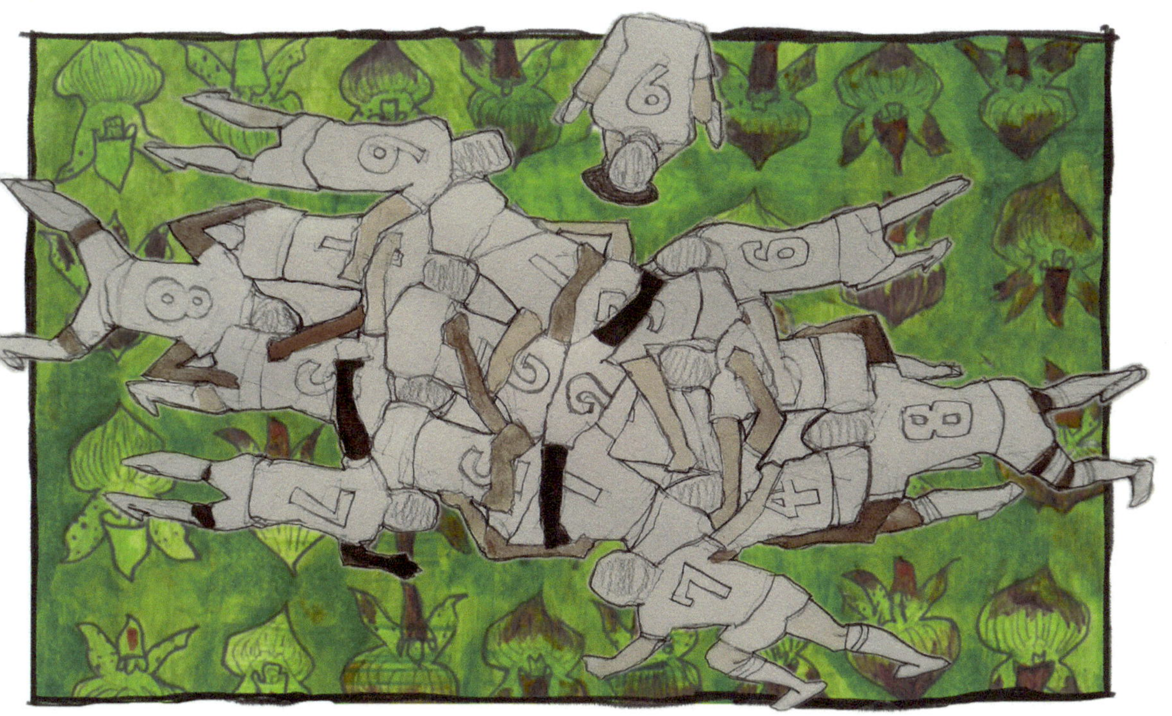

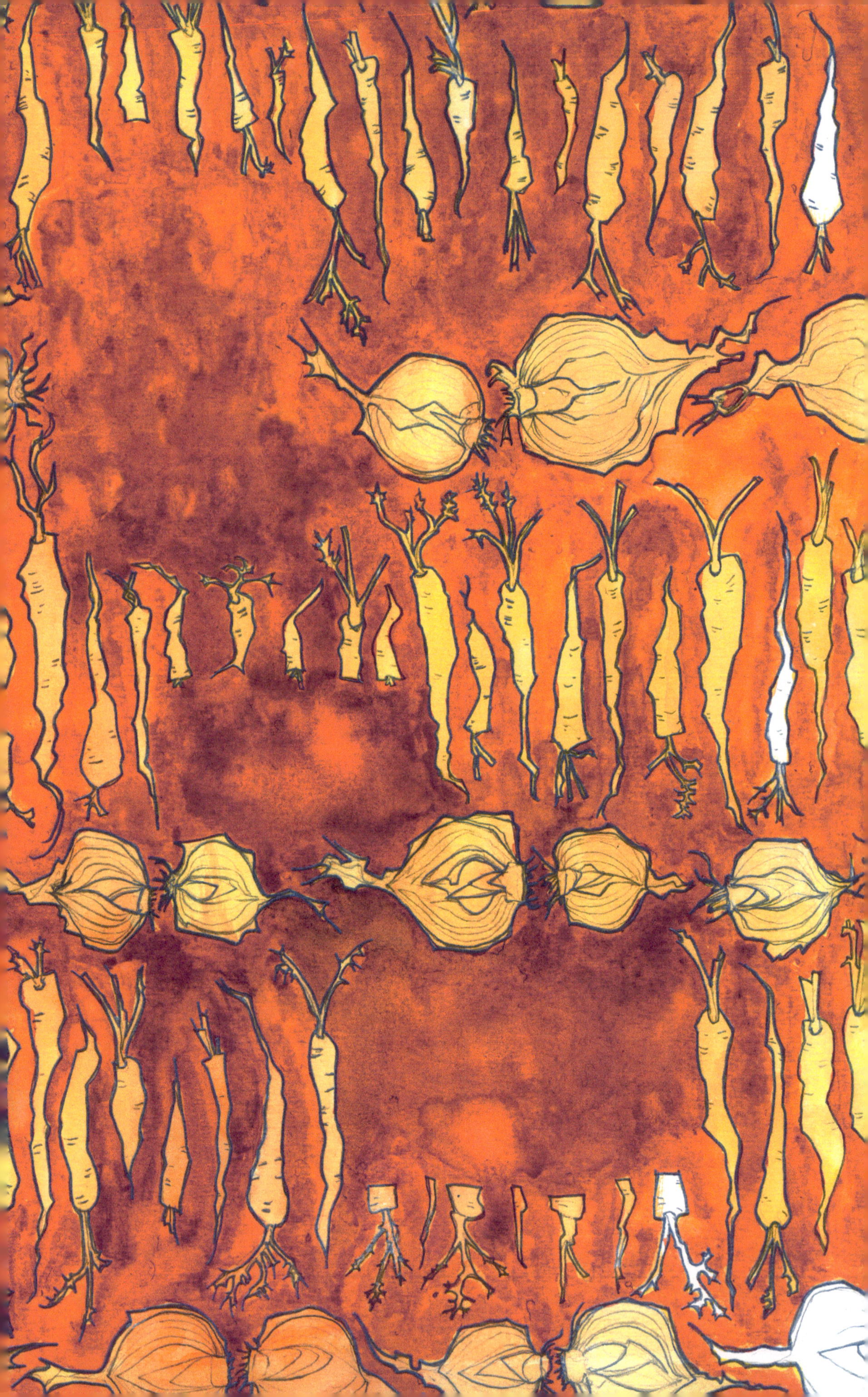

www.ingramcontent.com/pod-product-compliance
Lightning Source LLC
Chambersburg PA
CBHW041137260726
48664CB00027B/1273